Praise for

The Supreme Victory of the Heart

"Sharon Hewitt Rawlette has written one of the most courageous, captivating, and unflinchingly honest memoirs to appear in years. *The Supreme Victory of the Heart* explores the eternal question: Do we find love, or does love find us? I cannot imagine any reader whose life will not be enriched by this wonderful contribution."

– Larry Dossey, MD, *New York Times* best-selling author of *Healing Words* and *One Mind: How Our Individual Mind Is Part of a Greater Consciousness and Why It Matters*

"Heartfelt and inspirational, *The Supreme Victory of the Heart* is a deeply moving exploration of the mysteries of love, spirituality, philosophy, and life's purpose. What happens when the sacred love you've found forces you to question everything you've thought was true? Sharon Hewitt Rawlette bravely shares her pain and ultimately her triumph in healing and growing in love and awareness. ... Well-written and engaging, her story of life, love, and courage is inspirational and thought-provoking."

– Scarlett Heinbuch, PhD, author of *Waking Up to Love: Our Shared Near-Death Experience Brought Miracles, Recovery and Second Chances*

"As I absorbed the honesty and wisdom of this captivating memoir in a single sitting, I connected with a piece of my heart's experience that I hadn't even realised was missing: a profound and palpable example of the true nature of unconditional love. Not only did I read *The Supreme Victory of the Heart*, this book read me."

– Dr. Mary Helen Hensley, best-selling author of *Understanding Is the New Healing*, *Promised by Heaven*, and co-author of *Bringing Death to Life*

"I was immediately pulled into *The Supreme Victory of the Heart* by Sharon Hewitt Rawlette. The writing is gorgeous, and I was reminded that love is a great healer, but love also requires a spiritual perspective to see this play out over time. As Sharon writes, 'The thing is, love does turn out to be enough. It's not enough, maybe, to give us exactly the life we desire. It doesn't follow predictable, easily discernible patterns. But it does have this one predictable aspect: it will always take us somewhere good, even if that place is on the other side of tremendous pain.' I whole-heartedly recommend reading *The Supreme Victory of the Heart*. Read it on a plane, read it by the beach, or read it in bed on a rainy day. Sharon writes with great respect for the people in her story, and her attention to detail brings the story to life. Reading *The Supreme Victory of the Heart* will most likely help you feel greater compassion and love for yourself and others."

– Tricia Barker, author of *Angels in the OR: What Dying Taught Me About Healing, Survival and Transformation*

"*The Supreme Victory of the Heart* beautifully relays a story of personal growth and empowerment as Rawlette navigates uncertainty with grace. She keeps firm hold of the life learnings even while telling a synchronistic love story, so it is reaffirmed for me, the reader, that love of self comes before any other form of love."

– Sky Nelson-Isaacs, author of *Living in Flow: The Science of Synchronicity and How Your Choices Shape Your World*

About the Author

Sharon Hewitt Rawlette has a PhD in philosophy from New York University but left academia in 2010 to pursue creative writing and cottage farming. Her first mainstream publication was her 2011 *Salon* article "When my fiancé told me about the other woman," followed by personal essays in *Orion*, *The Baltimore Review*, and *BREVITY's Nonfiction Blog*. Since then, she's written extensively on the subject of coincidence and synchronicity: on her *Psychology Today* blog "Mysteries of Consciousness," in the peer-reviewed *Journal of Scientific Exploration*, and in her 2019 book *The Source and Significance of Coincidences: A Hard Look at the Astonishing Evidence*. With *The Supreme Victory of the Heart*, she returns to her first love—memoir—and shares with readers her debut encounters with the phenomenon of meaningful coincidence.

THE SUPREME VICTORY OF THE HEART

The Supreme Victory of the Heart

A Memoir of Love, Loss, and Synchronicity

SHARON HEWITT RAWLETTE

© 2020 by Sharon Hewitt Rawlette

All rights reserved. No part of this book may be reproduced in any form by any electronic or mechanical means without permission in writing from the author except in the case of brief quotations used in critical articles, reviews, and scholarly works. Correspondence regarding permission for reproduction may be addressed to the author at sharon.rawlette@gmail.com.

ISBN: 978-1-7339957-2-6

The following is a work of memoir. Some names and inessential details have been changed to protect the identities of persons involved. Also, while the author has done her best to stick as closely to the truth as possible, most dialogue has been recreated from memory and so should not be considered an exact transcription of the conversation in question.

Chapter ONE

It was 10pm for me, but four in the morning for my fiancé. Not a reassuring hour to get a phone call.

Until then, my Labor Day weekend had been positively dreamy. It was the first time I'd seen my family since getting engaged to Samuel in France over the summer, and we'd all driven down to Atlantic Beach, North Carolina, and spent the last two days bobbing in the waves, sipping strawberry daiquiris by the hotel pool, and eating as much fried seafood as our stomachs could handle.

Upstairs, the hotel room I was sharing with my sister and parents was an avalanche of wedding paraphernalia: French bridal magazines I'd picked up on my way through Charles de Gaulle Airport, stacks of library books on designing centerpieces and homemade wedding favors, pictures of my wedding dress I'd printed off the internet, and mock-ups of the invitation I was designing—shiny silver paper glued to an indigo background and decorated with snowflakes I'd meticulously stamped and embossed in the two days since I'd landed in the States.

I also had a manila folder bulging with triplicate copies of documents to submit to the French Consulate for my marriage visa: three months' worth of bank statements, a letter from Blue Cross Blue Shield describing my healthcare coverage abroad, my birth certificate (which still needed a special seal to make it valid internationally, but it was anyone's guess which government agency gave those out), and a letter from someplace called "Global Services," which assured the French government that I had purchased insurance for flying my body back to the States in the event that I died on French soil before becoming a permanent resident. Given the length of the process so far, that didn't seem entirely out of the question.

I knew from previous experience negotiating for student visas that this was only the beginning of my battle with *la bureaucratie française*, but frankly, I didn't care. It didn't matter how many times the folks at the French Consulate implied I was naïve to believe what they'd written on their website. I knew that all this red tape was just a rite of passage, the ceremony that—at the end of a few hellish months—would make me worthy of becoming an official member of French society.

On our last evening at the beach, my family drove over to New Bern to have some burgers with my aunt and uncle at a trendy spot downtown. We talked all about the wedding and how excited everyone was to have an excuse for planning a trip to France. The conversation was so animated that I didn't hear any of the three times my phone rang during dinner. And I didn't notice the missed calls until we got back to the hotel around ten.

My sister Sarah already had the TV on, flipping channels. Mom was folding back the comforter on her bed, and Dad was stepping onto the balcony to enjoy the cool night air and the sound of the waves seven stories below. I slipped off my shoes, dropped my purse into my open suitcase, and flipped open my phone to see who the missed calls were from. They were all from Samuel. And he'd left a voice message.

Just as I was about to dial voice mail, the phone rang again. "Hey," I answered, a bit concerned. Samuel wasn't the sort of person to stay up until four in the morning. Or lose sleep over trivialities. Or call repeatedly instead of waiting to be called back. "Sorry I didn't pick up before," I said. "I didn't hear the phone in the restaurant. What's up?"

"Sharon," he said, in a disturbingly serious voice.

I stepped into the bathroom and closed the door behind me. "What is it?"

"Are you sitting down?"

No, I was standing at the faux-marble sink, staring blankly into the mirror as my brain ran through the most likely catastrophes. Someone must have died. Or gotten cancer. Or severed multiple limbs. I closed the flimsy plastic lid of the toilet and lowered myself onto it. "Yes, I'm sitting down."

"Sha-*hone*," he said again, his French accent making the 'r' in my name sound like an 'h'. "I can't marry you."

We had been together for three years, but we'd known each other for nine. I had met Samuel on my very first trip to France, when I was studying abroad in college. I never would have dated him then, though. I was still a recovering evangelical Christian, steeped in a culture that said the earth was created in six days, the man was supposed to be the head of the household, and the most you could safely do before marriage was kiss. And even that, I wasn't entirely sure about. Clearly Frenchmen were out.

But time changes so many things. Six years later, I was solidly an atheist. An atheist struggling to make a life outside the reassuring walls of the church. And, for me, France seemed the natural place to do that.

My love affair with France had begun all the way back in childhood, when my parents would pepper their conversations with phrases they remembered from their high-school French classes: *s'il vous plaît, merci, bonne nuit.* I could tell how much my mother would have liked to speak French fluently, the way young women were always doing in Jane Austen novels, and I suppose she passed that longing on to me.

Then there was my Aunt Claire, married to my dad's brother. She'd been born in France, to missionary parents. Later she'd lived in Ivory Coast and Haiti. She *did* speak French. And made French coffee. And reminisced about French cheeses. On top of that, she was always chicly dressed, decorated her house with an impeccable mix of stainless steel and Old World antiques, and consistently served mouth-watering food. In my mind, her Frenchness was the root of all her other virtues.

When we went to my aunt and uncle's house for Thanksgiving or Christmas, it wasn't long before I'd head for the rack of French magazines they kept in the corner of the living room. I'd lay an issue of *Maison Française* open on the kitchen table and spend hours poring over its pages, trying to decipher the meanings of the photo captions—for instance, the difference between the words "*ci-dessus*" and "*ci-dessous*," two practically identical words that had opposite meanings: above and below.

When I was thirteen, my parents gave me a Céline Dion album in French: *Dion chante Plamondon*. Until then, the only French songs I knew featured Edith Piaf and/or the accordion. Now, sitting beside the Christmas tree with my Discman and headphones, I was surprised to hear drums, bass, and electric guitar—*real* music! Then Céline Dion came in singing an earnest, punchy melody. And it hit me for the first time that there were people who actually lived their *lives* in this language.

After much painstaking effort with a dictionary, I finally understood that the song *"Des mots qui sonnent"* was about a singer pleading with her songwriter to give her some hit lyrics. *"Le monde est stone"* was about giving up on the world and wanting to die. *"Oxygène"* was about a woman going through the motions of a life she didn't believe in and having a harder and harder time catching her breath. And then there was *"L'amour existe encore"*: love still exists.

The more I listened, the more the glorious pathos of Dion singing Luc Plamondon's lyrics merged with the French language. French became for me the language of someone singing for freedom, someone singing to express a self that for too long had been kept buried inside. And the fact that I could sing all of these songs without my parents' having a clue as to their meaning was, well, totally awesome.

I wasn't a particularly angst-ridden teenager. I took pride, actually, in being unlike the stereotypical high schooler and instead getting along great with my family. What angst I did feel in my teen years was due to spiritual things. My family was Southern Baptist, and while my parents were more liberal than a lot of the denomination—my sisters and I were allowed to listen to rock music and we were homeschooled by our own choice, not out of any desire by our parents to shelter us from the secular world—I had a streak of perfectionism that left me feeling strong pressure to please God in everything I did. I used to spend over an hour every morning reading my Bible and praying. And then I would still feel guilty when I moved on to doing my schoolwork.

French, I suppose, became an island of refuge in the midst of the pressure I put on myself to be a perfect Christian, a perfect daughter, and a perfect student. And when I finally got to France for the first time, for a semester in my junior year of college, the effect only increased. France was far enough, and different enough, from home to allow me to relax my attention to others' expectations. Sort out my own beliefs. And just maybe blossom into the sexy, dynamic woman I had always wanted to be.

Samuel and I didn't date during my first stay in France, but when I came back six years later during grad school, we did. And his love and companionship finally made me feel at home in my new secular, international life. He loved me the way I'd always longed for someone to. In fact, we were well-nigh inseparable. After we'd been together just a few weeks, there was no doubt in my mind that we were going to spend the rest of our lives at each other's side.

Samuel's family had a farm in Brittany, in western France, and spending summers there confirmed something else I had long suspected: that I was not a city girl at heart, even though, between New York and Paris, I'd been living in the city for four years. No, I was meant to live on a farm—meant to have my hands in the dirt, or gripping the smooth wooden handle of a pitchfork, or catching the evening's dinner by two scaly yellow legs. Emerging from the farmhouse on a cool June morning to a cloudless sky and the sound of a young rooster struggling to produce his first notes, I knew that I was in exactly the right place. Thousands of miles from the town where I was born, speaking a new language and learning new customs, I knew in my soul that I was home. When Samuel asked me to marry him, and his dad told us he was going to pass the farm on to us, there was nothing more I could have wished for. I had absolutely everything.

Which was why my excitement was running so high that evening at Atlantic Beach, before Samuel's revelation that he couldn't marry me brought it to a dead stop.

I forced myself to take a couple of slow, deep breaths. Then I asked Samuel, in a surprisingly calm voice, "Why not?"

"I just can't," he replied, his voice catching slightly on the last word. "I'm so sorry."

"Tell me what it is."

"Sharon," he sighed. "You're not going to be happy in France so far away from your family."

"We've talked about this," I said. "I've lived away from my family for *eleven years*. I know exactly what it's like, and I'll be fine. What I want is to be near *you*."

"But we're not going to have the money to fly back to the States every year. Not when we have kids."

Samuel had mentioned some of these financial worries a month ago, when he took me on an engagement trip to England and Wales and we spent an afternoon strolling the grounds of Lyme Park, the estate that appeared as Pemberley in the 1995 BBC version of *Pride and Prejudice*. We were working our way down a wooded trail that skirted the mansion when Samuel brought up the question of plane tickets. That summer, the cheapest Washington-Paris roundtrip I'd been able to find was $1200. So Samuel's worries weren't entirely irrational. Especially since, at present, both he and I were technically unemployed. A couple of years ago, he'd left his job doing marketing consulting to write books on the history of philosophy, and just that spring, I'd left my academic career with a plan to support myself through writing, farming, and teaching piano lessons. But none of these projects was producing a viable income yet. We were both still living off savings.

Tonight, I told him the same thing I'd said that day at Lyme Park: "We'll find the money. And if we don't, then some years we may just have to skip going to the States, and my family can come to France. It's not a reason for us not to get married."

"I'm just not sure you'll be happy."

"Samuel, I fully understand what I'm getting into. And I know, with my entire being, that *this is what I want*. A life with *you*. In France."

"I don't know," he said wearily.

When he'd raised these fears on our engagement trip, it had taken me only a few minutes to allay them. When we got back from the UK, he threw himself headlong into wedding planning: booking a venue, calling caterers. He even tried to buy a copy of *What to Expect When You're Expecting*, before I convinced him that could wait until I was actually pregnant. Now, though, he seemed so empty of life. So resigned to these problems' being insurmountable. "Please tell me why you think this is such a big deal," I said. "I thought we worked through all of this."

"I just don't think it's going to be right."

"Why not? I don't see how the things you're saying are suddenly so much more important."

"I can't marry you, Sharon," he repeated softly. "I'm really sorry."

What could I say? It was like there was suddenly this enormous wall between us. An enormous, explanation-repelling wall. "Well," I said, "what are we going to do?"

I expected Samuel to suggest that we put the wedding off for a few months, to give ourselves more time to think things over. Instead, he said very quietly, "Separate?"

I slid from the toilet to the floor. *Not again. Please not again.*

Images of another telephone conversation—on another floor—instantly filled my mind. That one had been a transatlantic call, too, but that time I'd been the one in France. When I went abroad in college, I was engaged to a guy I met at my Christian school. Then, a couple of months into my stay, I realized I'd become an atheist. With a heavy heart, I'd told Daniel, "I understand if you can't marry me anymore."

It had taken him a minute or two, but finally he said, "I'm not at the point where I need to break up with you over this."

I was surprised by such unconditional love. But I wanted it to be true, so I took him at his word. I assumed we were still on track to get married. However, soon after that, there started to be long pauses in our telephone conversations, especially when we talked about the future. During those pauses, I kept hoping to hear Daniel say, "I love you, Sharon. That's the one thing I know for sure. That I love you and will never leave you." I longed for him to utter those words of reassurance. But he never did.

In fact, the more I pushed him for some kind of security, the more he backed away. Until one day I had nothing more to say to him either. I just sat on the polished hardwood planks of my host parents' apartment floor and sobbed into the phone. I was the one who ultimately broke it off.

Now, on the floor of the bathroom in the Days Inn, the helplessness of that other period nine years ago came flooding back. I started crying and muttering things I couldn't rein in. "I can't believe this is happening again. I can't believe you're doing the same thing Daniel did. I thought this was different…I thought *we* were different. How can you *do* this to me?"

"I am *not* doing the same thing Daniel did," said Samuel, with a surprising amount of conviction.

"Then I don't understand. What's going on? Why can't you explain it to me?" I was blubbering now and couldn't be sure Samuel was actually catching everything I was saying, especially since it was in English.

"I'm going to hang up," he said. "I can't listen to you cry."

"No!" I barked, with as much authority as I could muster. I knew Samuel had a hard time listening to me cry over the phone. He had a very empathetic soul, and felt something akin to physical pain whenever he was helpless to comfort me four thousand miles away. But I simply could not bear for him to go at that moment. "Do *not* hang up," I repeated. "Do. Not. Hang. Up."

He stayed on the line. But then neither of us could find anything else to say. I had asked all of my questions and gotten the same unsatisfying responses every time. So we just listened to each other's breathing. After a couple of minutes, I felt a little more in control. "I guess we should say good night," I conceded.

"I think it's a good idea."

"I love you, Samuel."

"I love you, too, Sharon. Good night."

"Good night."

I laid my head against the bathroom door and closed my eyes.

I had waited so long to be engaged to Samuel. For the three years we'd been dating, I'd courageously borne up under my parents' disapproval of our living together and sleeping together because I knew that what we had was beautiful, pure, and good. But I also knew that it was going to take a wedding for my parents to see that. I had been so relieved when Samuel had finally been ready to marry me. And I had heard the joyous relief in my parents' voices when I announced the news to them over the phone. Now what was I supposed to do?

After ten minutes or so, I got to my feet and went out into the bedroom. Sarah and my parents were all under their covers, reading. I didn't look at anyone, just headed straight for my suitcase and pajamas.

"How's Samuel?" asked my mom.

"Not so good," I said, in a surprisingly steady voice. I immediately disappeared back into the bathroom to change. Of all the nights to get this news. When I had no privacy at all.

After brushing my teeth, I reemerged from the bathroom, lay my dirty clothes on top of my suitcase, and stoically slid into bed beside Sarah. I thought I might feel better once I was between the sheets with my head on the pillow, but as soon as I was horizontal, every negative emotion I'd been managing to keep at bay began rushing toward me. Apparently, the moments of calm I'd felt were the ocean receding from the beach in preparation for a tsunami. I needed to say something to my family before the wave swept me away. "Samuel doesn't want to get married anymore," I choked out, and immediately burst into tears.

My mother threw back her covers and came to my side, putting her hand gently on my back as I sobbed into the pillow. As difficult as my relationship with my mother had become since I'd left Christianity, I was relieved to know I could still count on her in such a desperate moment. "What happened?" she quietly asked.

"Nothing," I sputtered. "*Nothing* happened. I don't understand." I could hardly put a coherent thought together now. All I felt was an overwhelming sense of impending loss.

My mom rubbed my back. When she eventually got up to get a box of Kleenex from the bathroom, my sobs subsided into sniffles, and I sat up long enough to wipe the tears and snot from my face. She put the box of tissues next to me on the bedside table. "I love you, Sharon," she said and briefly touched my head. Then she slipped into her own bed next to my dad and turned off the lamp.

I fell asleep soon after that. Then a couple of hours later I was awake again, lying on my back with tears running from the corners of my eyes. I took a deep breath and turned onto my stomach. But the more I tried to suppress the tears, the worse they got. Soon everyone could hear me again.

My mother came back to my side. She lay down next to me and stroked my hair. "You just have to make it until morning," she whispered. "Then you can talk to him again."

It was true. I could talk to him again in just a few hours. And reassure him that, however much despair he was feeling right now, it didn't mean we had to separate. Samuel had his despairing moods, after all. When he was a child, he'd cried every Christmas when he opened his presents—because they were so beautiful, and he felt so loved, and for some reason he didn't think he deserved it all. Maybe tonight had just been one of his slumps. His fatalism might have led him to believe that, if he couldn't commit to marrying me now, there was no alternative besides separation. But I would assure him there was. I had already waited three years for him—more, if you counted the six years we were just friends. And with the love I felt for him, I knew I could wait many more.

True, the previous spring, I had given Samuel something of an ultimatum. I'd been in the process of leaving academia—a huge leap of faith for me, who for the last eleven years had always been associated with some university or another—and I was anxious to start my new life, by building a farm on a piece of land I could devote myself to for years to come. I wanted to be constructing fences, establishing asparagus beds, planting fruit and nut trees for the benefit of children and grandchildren. I wanted to be putting down very literal roots.

But I told Samuel I was willing to wait one more summer. I'd spend that summer with him in Brittany…as long as we stayed at his family's farm and not the beach house. I couldn't go another growing season without a vegetable garden and chickens. After that, it would be up to Samuel. If, by that fall, he was ready to get married, then we'd get married and establish a farm in France. But if he wasn't ready, then I was going back to the States to look for property to buy. He could come along, but if he decided later that he wanted to spend his life with me, it was going to have to be in the U.S.

Maybe it was the memory of that ultimatum that was making Samuel think we were going to have to separate. Yet now, faced with the very real prospect of losing Samuel, my need for a permanent place of my own lost its urgency. Yes, I needed to be outside, nurturing plants and animals and producing food by the sweat of my brow. But maybe I could keep doing that at Samuel's family farm for a little longer, even without the assurance that it would one day be my own. At this particular moment, mired in fear and worry, I was sure that I could muster all the patience in the world, as long as I got to keep Samuel in my life.

Eventually, my mom went back to bed. I tossed and turned for a long while, thinking that maybe if I found the right position, my body would relax into unconsciousness. But I only caught snatches of sleep for the rest of the night.

Finally, a faint glow shone through the crack between the hotel curtains. I slid quietly out of bed. I didn't have any minutes left on my international phone card, so I couldn't call Samuel from my cell, but there was no way I was going to wait to go out to a gas station and buy a new one. I carried the hotel phone through the sliding glass doors onto the balcony and unfolded a beach chair to face the eastern horizon. A thousand shades of yellow and pink were glowing in a show that seemed too beautiful for a world where this kind of heartache existed. I sat with the clunky old phone resting on my knees and felt my body relax into the knowledge that I was about to speak to Samuel.

I lifted the receiver and was set to dial when the door slid open behind me. My dad emerged. He went to the metal handrail and stood there, watching the sun rise.

"Can I talk to Samuel alone?" I finally asked him.

"I don't want you to be out here by yourself," he said. His head was turned in my direction, but he wasn't quite looking at me. I realized then that he was worried about the fact that we were seven stories off the ground and that, in a moment of desperation, I might do something irrevocable. His concern brought new tears to my eyes.

"Don't worry," I told him. "I'm not going to do anything stupid. I'm just going to stay sitting in this chair."

Without saying anything else, he went back inside and pulled the door shut behind him. I dialed Samuel's number.

"Hey, it's me," I said.

"Hey." He sounded as worn and pitiful as he had the night before. He might have gotten less sleep than I had.

"Samuel, I want you to know that we don't have to get married. We can stay unmarried and still be together."

There was no immediate response. Then he quietly said, "Okay." I'd been hoping for a little more. Hoping to hear some relief in his voice. But it would likely take both of us a while to recover from this scare. "When is your family leaving the beach?" he asked.

"This morning sometime. As soon as everybody's up and eats breakfast. Maybe around ten. But I can't talk long now. I had to call you on the hotel phone because my card's used up. I just wanted you to know that I love you, and we'll figure this out. Everything's going to be okay."

"All right. I'll call your *portable* later. When you're headed home."

It was a five-hour drive back to my parents' house in Virginia. I rode in the back seat with Sarah. While she watched *Grey's Anatomy* on her laptop, I looked out the window and tried to keep my tears as unobtrusive as possible. We stopped at Wendy's for lunch, and I ordered a junior cheeseburger but could only eat one bite. After that, I just stared at the table, using all my energy to will myself not to cry.

Back in the car, Mom tried to lighten the mood by putting U2's latest album in the CD player. What she didn't know was that that album had special meaning for me and Samuel. U2 had recorded *No Line on the Horizon* in Morocco in August 2007, the same month Samuel and I were in Morocco for a friend's wedding. We'd been dating all of three months at that point, though we acted like we'd been together forever. On a sightseeing trip to Meknès, a bunch of our friend's relatives were sitting around a café table over steaming mint tea, discussing the elaborate preparations for the wedding. It was going to take place in traditional Berber fashion, under tents carpeted with elaborate woven rugs. There'd be dancers and singers, and the bride was going to wear not one but five different gowns over the course of the night. A cousin leaned over to Samuel and asked, "Should we start making arrangements to throw one of these for you and Sharon?"

Samuel grinned. "Sounds good to me!"

The goodness of the memory made my heart ache all the more.

When Samuel discovered that U2 had recorded an album in Morocco the same month we were there, he bought it the very day it came out. On the night he brought it home to our apartment outside Boston (I was teaching at Brandeis University then), I annoyed him by reading the lyrics aloud, in a purposely ridiculous monotone. But I hadn't paid close attention to the words—until now, when Bono's voice filled the car singing "Moment of Surrender," with a line about entertaining doubts on the day of one's wedding.

I had long believed Samuel and I were different from most couples, or at least from the way I imagined most other couples to be. In my eyes, our story had always been a miraculous one. From our first, random encounter at the Université de Nancy nine years ago to the way we had just happened to both be living in Paris five years later. And the way our lives had suddenly meshed that following spring, when each of us discovered in the other a companion who understood our deepest thoughts and feelings. One morning, while lying next to each other in bed, we put our palms together and discovered that our hands were exactly the same size. "*On est jumeaux,*" Samuel had said. We're twins. I felt that our souls had been attached to each other long before our minds or our bodies.

And that was what enabled me not to worry for three years about whether we were going to get married. With Daniel, I'd been constantly plagued by the worry that we might not end up together. I'd craved reassurance. But with Samuel, I always felt a deep sense of peace. Truthfully, I believed we *were* married, on a level deeper than a lot of church marriages ever attained. We loved each other and knew each other so deeply and truly that we didn't need certainty about our earthly future together. We didn't need *promises*. What bound us to one another was something stronger than either of our wills.

But as I listened to U2 and contemplated the coincidence of hearing those lyrics on this particular day, I began to wonder whether, if the universe had given Samuel and me a love that was stronger than normal, it was because it had a task for us that was harder than normal, too. It may seem like a suspiciously spiritual line of thought for someone who had given up belief in God, but, listening to this album once again, I began to get the distinct impression that what Samuel and I were about to experience was of tremendous importance.

Samuel called me in the car on the way back from the beach. We talked pleasantly for a few minutes, but he still seemed unaccountably depressed. He didn't seem to be better the next day, either. Or the day after that. In fact, the entire week, he sounded like he was speaking from underneath a ton of bricks.

"Samuel," I finally said, "you know that I'm not just your lover, I'm your best friend. And I won't stop being your best friend even if you have something very difficult to tell me."

"Thank you," he replied. I thought I finally heard the relief I'd been waiting for. "Thank you for saying you're my friend. Because I *do* have something difficult to say. I've been writing and rewriting an email to you all week."

"You can tell me."

"I don't know," he hedged.

"I'm probably stronger than you think I am." In any case, I knew I'd be stronger if I wasn't left to imagine the worst. "Did you sleep with someone else?" I asked.

"No."

"Did you find out you have a child?" Once, I'd dreamt that his ex-girlfriend had shown up with a two-year-old she claimed was his.

"No, it's nothing that serious."

"Then what is it? Please just *tell* me."

"I'll finish the mail and send it to you tomorrow afternoon."

The next day was Saturday, and my parents and I had plans to go sailing. I was going to have to spend all day with them on a twenty-one-foot boat, trying to act happy while inside I was dying wondering what in the world Samuel had to tell me. But if this was the way he wanted to do it…okay.

The next morning dawned warm but not hot. We trailered the boat to a little bay on the south side of the Potomac River and put in at the public boat ramp. Once the sails were up, there was enough breeze to send us quickly across the river, four miles wide at that point. I sat for a long while on the metal railing at the bow, rising and falling as we slid over each successive wave, trying to absorb from the sun, wind, and waves the energy I was going to need to deal with whatever Samuel had to say. *My perfect Samuel. What could possibly be so wrong?*

When we finally got home in the late afternoon, my stomach was a bundle of knots. I went straight to the computer, still in my swimsuit and flip-flops. There was an email from Samuel, but it was only a couple of lines long. He said he hadn't been able to finish his email because his sister had just gotten back from a trip, and they'd spent the whole day together visiting with family.

I felt anger beginning to simmer inside me. Didn't Samuel understand how anxious I had been for the last twenty-four hours? Didn't he know that I'd only been able to act halfway sane because I knew that, when I got home, I would finally have some answers? How could he keep drawing this out?

But, as angry as I was, I realized that Samuel would only be doing this if what he had to say was *really* hard for him—if he was even more scared than I was. I wrote back to him, telling him not to be afraid. "I think I'm stronger than you believe," I said. "I'm listening. Ready for anything."

The next morning, we spoke briefly on the phone before Samuel had to go to his aunt and uncle's for lunch. "I didn't want to send my mail yesterday because it was September 11th," he said. "I didn't want it to turn to disaster. But I promise I'll write you this evening. If you'll make me a promise."

"What?"

"Promise not to read my mail until you're alone in your room, ready to go to bed."

My stomach hurt thinking about the implications of this. "Okay, I promise."

"I'll call you at seven tomorrow morning," he said.

At ten o'clock that evening, I said good night to my parents and shut the door to my bedroom—which truthfully was hardly a bedroom anymore. It was more of a store room for everything Samuel and I had moved out of our apartment in Massachusetts and were waiting to ship to France. Half the room was stacked with cardboard boxes full of philosophy books, dishes, and kitchen appliances. Before going to the beach, I'd been sorting through them, pulling out things that were small enough to be packed into my suitcase. Now they were just cluttering the floor, waiting for their fate to be determined.

On the other side of the room, in an alcove, was the queen-size mattress Samuel and I had shared in Massachusetts. It sat on the floor in front of a couple of bookcases where I'd unpacked only my most essential volumes: Nancy Huston, Wendell Berry, and Helen and Scott

Nearing's homesteading classic *The Good Life*. The mattress was covered with the blue and white quilt I'd once made with the hope that Daniel and I would use it when we got married. As I sat down on it now, I noticed that several of the seams were starting to fray.

I pulled my laptop over from where it was sitting against the wall and signed in to Hotmail. Samuel's promised email was at the top of my inbox.

It began with the words, "There is a girl."

Chapter TWO

This girl was an old friend of Samuel's. He had known her for fifteen years, since high school. Strange that this was the first I'd heard about her. Then again, maybe it wasn't that strange.

High school had been a troubled time for Samuel. I'd heard bits and pieces of the story over the three years we'd been a couple, but not until the previous summer had I seen Samuel get emotional about it.

We were sitting in the kitchen of his childhood home. It was a typical farmhouse kitchen, with counters around two sides, a pantry along a third, and the table in the middle, covered in a vinyl table cloth that Samuel's dad meticulously wiped down after every meal. That table was the center of the household. The place where all the deep discussion happened. On winter evenings, Samuel, his dad, and I would sit around the table for hours, slowly sipping our puréed squash soup and discussing the state of the world: the endangered Breton dairy industry, the threat of cheap Brazilian poultry, the wild fluctuations in the price of wheat due to speculators on the stock exchange thousands of miles away in Chicago.

If anyone happened to mention anything related to health or medicine, Samuel's dad would eagerly contribute some tidbit of naturopathic knowledge he'd learned from his wife. *"Ma femme était très intéressée par ces choses,"* he'd remind me. My wife was very interested in these things. Samuel, on the other hand, was not. *"Les choses matérielles,"* he called them. Material things. When the conversation turned to anything mundane or down-to-earth, Samuel would quickly finish eating and head upstairs to his computer to write another chapter of whatever philosophy book he was currently working on.

Once Samuel was out of the room, his dad would often start opening up about Samuel's mother. *"C'était une femme impressionnante,"* he would say, with a smile that showed he was trying to be humble but couldn't quite contain his admiration for his wife. "She was an impressive woman. She could make anyone feel at home at this table. And she loved to get people talking about themselves and their pasts. She always cut right to the chase. There was no fooling Angèle. She asked very pointed questions."

Sometimes this would lead to a discussion of marriage. *"Le mariage est une grande aventure,"* he'd say. Marriage is a great adventure. "The most important thing is that each person helps the other to grow."

I would nod my head in agreement. "Samuel has helped me grow tremendously. You and your wife have raised a truly wonderful son." Sometimes tears would pool in my eyes as I said this, because I wished I could have spoken these words to Samuel's mother as well. But she had passed away from cancer two months before I visited his family for the first time.

One afternoon during the summer of our engagement, Samuel and I were sitting alone at the kitchen table. We'd been working outside that day—cutting firewood, I think. Cool weather came early to Brittany, and sometimes we would build a fire even in August. Now we were resting our weary arms and legs and enjoying a cup of the mint tea Samuel's dad liked to buy from the organic co-op. Samuel was looking a little glum, as he always did on days when he was forced to work with his hands instead of his brain. But this time it seemed like something else might be bothering him. "What's wrong?" I asked.

"I'm just thinking about my friend," he said, fingering the handle of his mug.

"The one who died?"

"*Oui.*"

When Samuel was in high school, a good friend of his had passed away. I wasn't sure how. I just knew that Samuel got very quiet on the rare occasions when the subject came up.

"Can you tell me what happened?" I asked.

"It's not easy to explain," he said. He looked away, and I thought that might be the end of it. But after a moment he went on.

In fits and starts, intermingled with tears, Samuel began to tell me stories about this friend. I had to admit that I did indeed have trouble making sense of a lot of what he said, but what was clear was the strong emotional impact of the experiences they had shared and the lasting effect that the unexpected death of this friend had had on Samuel.

At one point, I scooted my wooden chair over next to him and pulled him into my arms, letting him weep into my shoulder. Whatever the ultimate significance of all this, Samuel had badly needed to share it.

"Thank you for telling me this," I said, squeezing his hand in mine. "I don't understand it all, but it's something I needed to know about you. I need you to keep talking to me like this."

Samuel nodded.

Our conversation soon moved on to other things, and I didn't hear any more about the subject until a month or so later when Samuel sent me his devastating email. The "girl" he spoke of was a friend of his from high school. She had been in the same circle of friends as the guy who died. And she had experienced the same difficult events that Samuel had.

Samuel confessed he'd been interested in her. And that she'd been interested in him. But neither of them had been aware of the other's feelings.

My heart was sinking, but I read on. Samuel explained that he hadn't seen this girl frequently since high school. They'd gone a few years without seeing each other when he saw her again at his mother's funeral. A few months after that, she broke up with her boyfriend, and they saw each other once more. They talked about their common past. "Nothing happened," wrote Samuel.

After that, he said, they sporadically exchanged emails. One email a year ago. Then one this past April. She wanted to see him. She'd just lost someone else close to her. But they stuck to corresponding. Only towards the end of the summer did Samuel agree to meet up with her. After I went back to the States.

It was the first time they'd seen each other in four years. They had dinner together and discussed the events of the past once again. Each of them discovered things they'd never known before. A few days after that, they saw each other again and talked late into the night.

"This girl is back in my life," wrote Samuel.

His words made my heart catch in my throat. And there were still several paragraphs to go.

Samuel said that he felt he'd left a part of himself back in high school. He mentioned his deceased friend again. He also mentioned God. "God is back in this story," he wrote, with unusual theological directness. It wasn't like Samuel to speak so blatantly about the workings of the divine.

I knew Samuel was a Christian, of course. Sort of. One of his favorite sayings was, *"Dieu n'existe pas, et il s'en fout."* God doesn't exist, and he doesn't give a damn. When Samuel and I had first crossed paths nine years before at the Université de Nancy, he'd been astonished to meet an American atheist, and I'd been astonished to meet a French Christian. We'd spent a long time trying to explain our positions to each other. But, over the years, I'd come to believe that our beliefs were more alike than different. If Samuel believed in God, it wasn't the personal God I'd grown up with, the one you were supposed to chat with as if he was your best friend. It seemed like Samuel believed in God more as a meaningful force behind the universe. And that was something I thought I could live with.

But now, with this email, Samuel began talking about God in much more personal terms. He wrote to me that he believed it was God who had brought the two of us together when we'd begun dating three years before, and that just as God had been calling us to live something special then, God was now calling us on to something new and different.

What worried me most was not the fact that Samuel was deferring to the will of a divine being, but the fact that this God he spoke of appeared not to have Samuel's best interest at heart. The overriding tone of Samuel's email was one of angst and suffering, of being pulled apart against his own desires. He'd wanted to marry me, he said. He'd wanted to stop thinking and reflecting so much and start simply living. "You are all that I need," he said at one point. He mentioned our spiritual relationship—the deep spiritual connection he and I had both felt from early on. "That does not change," he said.

Nevertheless, something had happened that he hadn't expected. Something that completely upended his plans. God was back. This girl was back. This *friend* was back, in some obscure way that appeared to torment him. Was the torment just his desire not to cause me suffering? I couldn't tell, but it seemed deeper. He seemed to be talking about hurts from his past. Hurts that wouldn't let him go.

The email didn't wrap anything up neatly. Toward the end, Samuel confessed that he felt torn in two. Then he said, "I can not finish that mail. I do not like it." The email ended right there. Samuel hadn't even signed it.

I didn't cry. Maybe because the shock was too great. I read the email again and again. Each time slower, each time absorbing more. Samuel had kept this inside for a week and a half. Afraid of hurting me. Afraid of permanently ruining everything we'd built together, everything we were planning for our future.

At least now everything was out. It was a blow, to be sure. But at least now his severe anxiety made sense. Now I knew what was going on with my precious Samuel.

"Thank you for having the courage to tell me," I typed back to him. "Because now we can talk about things and decide together what to do. Remember that before anything else I'm your friend, and I love you no matter what. Only God knows whether we are supposed to be husband and wife, but we'll work together to figure out our next step. I love you."

I was grateful that Samuel had made me promise not to read his email until I was in bed. All I had to do after hitting "send" was close the computer, turn off the lamp on the bookshelf above my head, and slide under the quilt.

So this was the test God had for us. For me. God in the sense of "the Universe." The universe was offering us a chance to prove our love. To demonstrate just how deep it ran.

Chapter
THREE

If I believed Samuel and I had the ability to overcome such a great hurdle, it was in part because our relationship had always had an element of the miraculous. An undertow of destiny. As though, despite enormous odds, something was pulling us irresistibly together.

To start with, there was the way we'd met, nine years ago in the city of Nancy.

During my college semester abroad, I took some philosophy courses at the Université de Nancy. One of them was called "Intuition in Kant"—a funny coincidence, given the bit of personal intuition that came to me on the second day of class. That day, as the other students were stamping out their cigarettes in the hallway and trickling into the room, I noticed, in a seat across the room from me, someone who hadn't been at our first class session. Someone with a big shock of unruly black hair and a goatee. Think tortured intellectual. Or Russian anarchist. For some reason, I immediately thought to myself, *That's somebody I'd like to get to know.*

But I had no real expectation of becoming friends with him. I'd been in France for almost two months at that point and hadn't made a single French acquaintance—apart from my host parents, who got paid to be nice to me. All the French students at the university were too well established in their social circles to concern themselves with a foreigner. Before class, they huddled in little groups in the hallway, smoking and laughing at jokes with too much slang in them for me to understand. The only time I got up the courage to speak was in class, and then I knew my heavy American accent scared away most potential friends.

Well, that day after class, I was approached for the very first time by a French student. And it just happened to be the fellow with the wild black hair. "*Bonjour. Moi, c'est Samuel. Tu viens d'où?*"

Where are you from? he was asking. For once my accent seemed to have elicited positive interest. "*Je suis américaine*," I replied.

"What part of the States are you from?" he asked.

"About an hour south of Washington. Have you been to the U.S.?"

"*Non*, but I studied in Scotland. In Dundee."

"Ah." I nodded in feigned recognition.

The classroom was quickly clearing out. I took a step toward the door, and Samuel followed. Soon, we were walking side by side down the worn, cigarette-strewn linoleum of the hallway. "How long are you in France?" asked Samuel.

"Till January."

"You're a philosophy student?"

"*Oui*." I had only changed my major from music that past spring, but yes, I was officially in philosophy now.

As we reached the stairwell leading down to the first floor, Samuel turned to me. "Would you like to go to lunch?" he asked.

Never in my life had I been asked to a meal by someone I'd just met. Not even my fiancé Daniel—who didn't have a shy bone in his body—had been that quick to ask me out. Did Samuel mean it like a date?

"Sure," I said, trying to act nonchalant, like this sort of thing happened to me all the time. But I wished for the first time that I had an engagement ring. I'd told Daniel not to buy me one, so we could save what little money we had for more practical things like rent, but it would have been nice to have some unobtrusive way of showing Samuel I was taken.

On our way across campus, Samuel stopped at a phone booth to make a call. It was 2001, and cell phones were still few and far between. I had on a birthstone ring my mother had given me, and while I waited for Samuel, I took it off my right ring finger and slid it onto my left. Just in case.

Samuel took me to the campus dining hall, one of those bastions of French studentdom I hadn't dared to enter on my own. Samuel slipped me one of his meal tickets at the door, and shook his head when I tried to hand him a few francs to pay him back.

The place was packed, but we squeezed into a couple of seats across from each other at a long rectangular table. A couple of Samuel's friends were sitting nearby, and we chatted with them for a bit. Or rather, I *tried* to chat. But I was much better at understanding one French person at a time. I found myself hoping that Samuel's friends would soon finish eating and leave. Only after they did did I realize how much pressure it could be to have Samuel's full attention!

"*Qu'est-ce que tu penses de la France?*" he asked. What do you think of France?

"*Je l'adore,*" I said. "*Vraiment.*" How could you not love a country with such absurdly good cafeteria fare? Roasted pork, braised vegetables, a crusty roll with camembert.... "But it's funny," I added, "because as much as I studied French in school, I hardly knew anything about French culture before I got here."

"What do you notice is different from the States?"

"Hm. I think the first thing I noticed is actually how similar they are. I thought France would feel exotic or something, but basically, it's the same as home. It's just small things that are different. Like the language. Or the fact that people kiss each other to say hello here." I thought about my first night I'd stayed with my host family, when my host sister's boyfriend greeted me with a kiss on both cheeks. He was three years older than I was and smelled better than anyone I'd ever met. I'd blushed beet red.

"How do you say hello in the States?" asked Samuel.

"We shake hands. Or we might hug if we haven't seen someone for a long time. But mostly we just say 'hi' and that's it."

"What other differences?"

"*Je ne sais pas.*" I looked around the cafeteria. "French women dye their hair a really strange shade of purple."

"Really?"

"Yeah. What you see everywhere in the streets here. I've never seen anyone's hair that color before. Or the pointy-toed shoes. That's got to hurt."

I was sure Samuel was just waiting for me to finish eating so he could say goodbye to the girl who thought purple hair and pointy shoes were the biggest cultural differences between the U.S. and France. But when we slid our trays into the conveyor belt at the back of the cafeteria, he surprised me by asking if I wanted to go get coffee.

We went to a nearby café, and Samuel ordered us espressos that came in two tiny porcelain cups, each with a chocolate-covered almond on the side. Samuel asked me about my philosophy program back at Messiah College—who I was reading, what my professors had written, what I thought my specialty would be if I went to graduate school. Eventually, I relaxed enough to notice his incredibly blue eyes.

"I have a meeting with a professor downtown," Samuel told me as we got up to go. "I was going to walk through the Vieille Ville. Have you ever been there?"

Actually, the Vieille Ville—Old Town—was the neighborhood where I'd stayed the first night I arrived in Nancy. But I shook my head.

"Let me give you the tour then," he said.

We stepped out of the café to find the sky filling ominously with clouds. Nevertheless, we headed for the Vieille Ville at a leisurely pace, Samuel pointing out significant landmarks along the way. When it began to rain, he pulled an umbrella from his bookbag. It was small, but he held it over both of us. We walked with our shoulders touching.

As we rounded a corner, I caught sight of two American girls from my exchange program standing across the street under their own umbrella, smiling at us. "There goes Sharon with her French boyfriend!" I heard one of them say in an unnecessarily loud voice. Didn't they know he could probably understand them? I didn't look at Samuel for fear he would see how red my face was.

But that was it. After that little walk, Samuel went off to his meeting, and the next week he wasn't in class. In fact, he never came back to Intuition in Kant again. Years later, he told me he had never planned to attend regularly, just to check it out once to see what it was like. Which made our meeting that day all the more lucky. What if he had never come to that class at all? And what if, on the particular day he was there, I hadn't spoken up and revealed my accent? What if I hadn't had such a clear view of him across the classroom—to help me decide, even before he approached me, that he was someone I wanted to get to know?

As it was, Samuel and I had exchanged email addresses, and a few weeks later we decided to have lunch again. This time at a pizzeria around the corner from campus. I was a lot more relaxed at this meeting, and according to Samuel, I spent most of the meal talking about my increasingly difficult issues with my still-fiancé Daniel. "I was disappointed to be stuck in the role of confidant," Samuel told me later. The funny thing is, *I* don't remember discussing Daniel at all. I remember talking about religion: discovering that Samuel called himself a Christian and telling him that I was not one. Anymore.

Samuel and I only saw each other one more time that semester, when we passed each other on the street down the hill from campus. Samuel seemed to be in a hurry, so I didn't keep him.

In any normal story, that would be all she wrote: the exchange student returns home and she and her casual French acquaintance send a couple of emails but then lose touch. And yet, for some reason I could never quite put my finger on, Samuel and I *didn't* lose touch. We regularly sent each other email updates every few months. For instance, I told Samuel when I spent a summer at the University of Notre Dame studying with the philosopher Alvin Plantinga, and he told me when he left philosophy and moved to Québec to work on an MBA. (He *didn't* tell me he moved there for a girl. I drew that conclusion myself when I got a mass email informing me that "Samuel et Catherine" had a new address....)

A year or so after Samuel moved to Canada, I moved to Manhattan, to do my doctorate in philosophy at NYU. When I'd been there for a couple months, Samuel wrote to say that he and some Canadian friends were taking a bus trip down to New York—would I like to meet up? I was frankly delighted at the thought of a visitor. I'd been discovering it was even harder to make friends in New York than in France, especially if you didn't particularly enjoy hanging out in bars. I spent a lot of evenings alone in my apartment, reading novels and listening to Norah Jones sing "Come Away with Me." And so when Samuel said he was coming to the city, I gladly offered him my couch if he needed a place to crash. To my surprise, he took me up on it.

I met him on a Friday evening at the front door of the NYU philosophy building. "Where are your friends?" I asked, after we'd given each other the obligatory *bisous* on both cheeks.

"Uptown at a hostel. I'll meet back up with them Sunday morning," he said.

Well, all right then. It seemed I was more central to Samuel's New York plans than I'd anticipated.

We dropped Samuel's pack off at my apartment, said hi to my roommate as she was leaving for the weekend, and headed out to a Thai restaurant for dinner. "*A moins que tu n'aimes pas la cuisine thaïlandaise*," I told him.

"Thai is great. I'm in New York; I want to try something new. By the way...your French is very good."

"*T'es trop flatteur*," I said, narrowing my eyes at him in mock suspicion. I knew very well what my French sounded like after two years of zero practice. My tongue was rejecting half the movements I tried to get it to make. And after just thirty minutes of conversation, I felt a headache coming on.

"It's true!" Samuel insisted. "Yes, your accent is a little rough, but the surprising thing is, you *think* in French. You're not just translating your English expressions."

"Hm." Maybe it was a genuine compliment after all.

After dinner, I took him to a French bar in the East Village. It was Halloween, and we sat at a sidewalk table watching superheroes and Playboy bunnies go past. Our waitress—Catwoman—did a rather suggestive dance on top of the bar.

"You know, it's funny," said Samuel, "but I have the impression I'm in France here." I assumed he didn't mean because of Catwoman.

I nodded. "Me, too." I think it was the narrow street, and all the people on the sidewalk.

We stayed out until midnight, talking philosophy and France. When we got back to my place, I helped Samuel scoot my two dormitory-issue loveseats together to form a very short bed. I handed him a pile of blankets and pillows. "I'm sorry I don't have something better to offer you."

"*C'est super. Vraiment.*"

The next morning, Samuel wanted to get an early start seeing Battery Park and the Statue of Liberty, so I told him I'd meet him after lunch in Central Park. Unfortunately, I was worried about the limitations of my grad-student budget, so instead of springing for the subway, I walked all the way from the Village to Midtown. And grossly underestimated the time it would take. Just as I was approaching the southeast corner of the park—a full thirty minutes late—my cell phone rang.

Just as I heard Samuel's worried voice asking me if everything was all right, I spotted him standing ten feet in front of me at a pay phone.

"*Je suis désolée,*" I said, tapping him on the shoulder. "Let me buy you a beer."

We got a couple of Heinekens in a café by Sheep Meadow and drank them outside while listening to a jazz combo. After that, we toured the park. At Strawberry Fields, we wondered aloud how to get to the Dakota Hotel, and a passerby gave us directions—in French.

As night began to fall, we headed back downtown, through Times Square. I pointed out the NASDAQ sign and mentioned that Daniel's engineering firm had helped design it.

"How *is* Daniel?" asked Samuel.

"He's all right. We're not together. We broke up while I was in Nancy."

"Was it hard?" he asked. "The break-up?"

"Sort of. But kind of a relief, too. It'd been coming for a while, and I was happy to have it over with."

"I remember you were suffering quite a bit."

"Really?" I had no idea that Samuel had been that tuned in to what was going on with me. "Well, not anymore. Daniel lives in Philadelphia, and things are fine the way they are."

Samuel stopped a couple of Chinese tourists who were going past and asked them to take a picture of us in front of the lights of the square.

By the time we'd slogged down through Madison Square Park and reached the East Village, we were so worn out from walking that I proposed we stay in for dinner. "What do you think about spaghetti?"

"Sounds good to me. Is there a place we can stop and get a bottle of wine?"

"There's a wine store on First Avenue. But I don't have a corkscrew."

Samuel smiled at the quaintness of my alcohol-deprived lifestyle. "I'll buy you one," he assured me.

We cooked the pasta together in my tiny kitchen, Norah Jones crooning in the background. Despite the cramped quarters, we managed to make a homemade marinara sauce and some fresh garlic bread, using the gas broiler in the oven. As I was rearranging the bread on the cookie sheet, Samuel was in the midst of stirring the noodles. Our arms briefly brushed against one another, and I felt it all the way to my toes.

We set our meal out on the little round table that NYU stocked in all their student apartments. Before we could comfortably eat, I had to level it with a piece of wadded-up cardboard. Then I gladly sat down and sipped the glass of Chianti that Samuel had filled to the brim for me. I listened to him wax poetic about my life in New York, where, according to him, I was destined to become a philosophy superstar.

"Nothing could be further from the truth," I told him. "I never have anything to say in seminars, even though I read the assignments three times before I go."

"*Parler beaucoup n'est pas la même chose que d'avoir de bonnes idées,*" he reminded me. Talking a lot is not the same as having good ideas.

This man was so full of compliments.

When we'd finished eating, Samuel wandered across the living room to browse my DVD collection. "I've never seen Baz Luhrmann's *Romeo and Juliet*," he said. "Is it good?"

"Very."

"Do you want to watch it?"

As I put the DVD in, Samuel sat down on the loveseat that was nearest to the TV, clearly leaving a place for me to sit next to him. I took it, but sat as close to the armrest and as far from him as possible. Somewhere along the way, the day seemed to have taken on a romantic cast, and my Christian-college self was rather worried about Samuel's expectations. Whatever they were, I felt in no position to live up to them. I was single now, yes, but I had only kissed one man in my entire life. And even though I had given up the conservative theology of my youth, I was having trouble shaking the conservative morals. I still believed sex was best saved for marriage—not a view I had ever heard a Frenchman espouse.

In fact, that afternoon over our beer in Central Park I had mentioned to Samuel a friend of mine whose wedding was a few months away. "I don't think I'll ever get married," Samuel had said. Maybe not, but I was under no illusion that he planned to be celibate. Not when he had once moved house with someone named Catherine.

And, frankly, I had no idea how to act with someone whose rules of engagement were so foreign to mine.

Things went all right for the first half of the movie, but when Leonardo DiCaprio and Claire Danes started making out in the swimming pool, I was suddenly ten times more aware of Samuel's presence than I had been at any other point during the day. I started to get prickles on the back of my neck and down my arms. I could feel my pulse quickening. Was this movie having the same effect on Samuel as it was having on me? Heaven help me!

I had no idea how to deal with the profound awkwardness this movie was spawning, so I did the only thing I could think of. I kept my gaze directed squarely at the television set and my body plastered against the armrest. It wasn't until the final scene of the movie that I dared to change my position slightly. That's when I felt for the first time Samuel's arm resting on the couch cushion behind me. When on earth had he put that there?

For the briefest of moments, I wondered what would happen if I turned toward him, if I chose to meet his gaze. If only I didn't have so little confidence in my ability to deal with a man untrained in Puritanism! If Samuel had gone to Messiah College, I could have kissed him and not had to worry about him wanting anything more. But a Frenchman…. That was completely out of my comfort zone.

Even when the credits rolled, I resisted turning to look at him. "What did you think?" I asked, striving to make my tone as academic as possible.

"*C'était bien.*"

"Good. Glad you liked it." I jumped up from the couch and made a beeline for my room. "Good night," I chirped, and shut the door securely behind me.

Fortunately, the morning sun streaming through the branches of the oak trees outside my apartment window made Samuel's presence seem much less threatening. I made us some mid-morning pancakes, and we had time for a leisurely brunch before he had to meet his friends at the bus. He asked if I had a map of Manhattan, and we spread it out on the table to retrace our steps of the day before.

"You know," I told him, still in French, "I've never heard you speak in English."

"*Si, j'en suis sûr,*" he replied. Yes, you have, I'm sure of it.

"No, you've always spoken French with me."

He looked down at the map. And then, in English, he said softly, "It's because I am shy about my English."

"Why?" I exclaimed. "You have a wonderful accent!"

He shrugged. "We made all this trip?" he asked, running his finger across the map from the Upper West Side to the East Village. His blend of French and Scottish sounds, and French and English grammar, was among the sexiest things I'd ever heard.

When we finally put the map away, Samuel leaned back in his chair and switched into French again. "*Dis-moi ce que t'en penses,*" he said. Tell me what you think. "Does a woman need a man to feel complete?"

We'd discussed a lot of philosophical topics over the last day and a half, but this was a new one. "*Je sais pas,*" I replied, as casually as I could manage. "I think a lot of women do. More than men, at least."

"I think it's the other way around," said Samuel. "I think men need women more. A man without a woman doesn't feel fully himself."

This didn't seem to be true of the guys I'd known. Daniel, for one, had always seemed thoroughly capable of getting along without me. But it was intriguing to think it might be true of Samuel.

We went back to talking about New York for a bit, and then Samuel abruptly changed the subject again. "*Si j'étais à New York,*" he said, "*est-ce que tu m'accepterais comme petit ami?*" If I was living in New York, would you accept me as a boyfriend?

I'm sorry—*what?*

I had no idea where to go with this question. It was phrased hypothetically, but something told me it had a direct relationship to the here and now. I searched for an evasive yet flirty response, but I was too flustered to be clever.

"No," I finally replied, settling on the most unsexy response I could possibly have mustered. "You don't want to get married, and I do. And I don't think it's a good idea to date people who don't have the same expectations." It was a line that could have come straight out of the Christian courtship manuals Daniel and I had pored over during our freshman year of college.

Thankfully, it was soon time for Samuel to go. He slung his army surplus pack onto his shoulder and stepped toward me. "*Merci beaucoup, Shahone.*" He kissed me on both cheeks and gave me a hug before heading to the elevator.

I didn't think much about Samuel for the next two years. His visit to New York had been flattering, and rather exhilarating at moments, but I never imagined its having a sequel.

At the same time, I did find myself waxing nostalgic for France. I started regularly watching the French news on public television and missing the silliest things about my days in Nancy: the need to walk around cars parked on the sidewalk, the pizzeria where the waiter continually encouraged me to substitute wine for a Coke at no extra charge, even the smell of cigarette smoke. In New York, I would sometimes follow a smoker a block or two out of my way just to keep breathing the scent that I remembered so vividly from the Université de Nancy.

Finally, I decided it was ridiculous to give myself lung cancer in New York when I could do it in France instead. It had been four years since I'd come back from Nancy, and even though my grad student stipend was small, I'd managed to save up a little money, what with all my refusing to take the train and eating homemade bean burritos for every other meal. (My roommate was a big fan of that dietary choice. Especially since I cooked the beans at eight in the morning, before class.) So in my third year of grad school, I decided to treat myself to ten days of Christmas break in Paris.

I figured Samuel was still in Canada, slaving over quarterly reports, or whatever it was MBAs slaved over. But I wrote him an email about my plans just in case. He quickly replied to say he was actually back in France, because his mother was sick with cancer. "I'm not sure what the situation will be when you come in December," he said, "but stay in touch." A few weeks later, when I wrote him with the exact dates of my flights, I found out his mother had just passed away. "But maybe you would like come to Brittany and stay with my family for a few days?" he said.

It was chilly the morning in early January that Samuel picked me up at the train station in Rennes, Brittany's capital city. As I rode the escalator up to the arrivals hall, I worried that I wouldn't recognize him after all this time. In fact, his hairstyle had calmed somewhat since the last time I'd seen him, but as it happened, I had no trouble at all picking him out. Before he even turned around, I recognized the curve of his shoulders. "*Salut, Samuel.*"

"*Salut, Shahone.*"

I was traveling with a college friend, Jeannette, and Samuel drove us both out of the city and through the foggy countryside to the little village where he was born. I could scarcely believe the charm spread out in front of me. Samuel pulled the car through a narrow alleyway into a paved courtyard, and there stood a house that looked like it had been lifted directly from a postcard: cream-colored stucco with red shutters and a slate roof, illuminated by the first rays of morning sun that managed to meander through the clouds.

Samuel gave us a tour, explaining that the house was from at least the early eighteenth century and that, when it was first built, only the center section was a dwelling. The wings had housed the horses and pigs, who apparently helped heat the house in winter. Over the years, though, the family expanded into the animals' quarters. And when Samuel's parents inherited the place from his grandparents, they did such a thorough makeover you would have thought the house had been designed as one great manor to begin with. Its walls were made of a mixture of clay and straw called *torchis* (a material detail supplied by Samuel's father), and they were almost two feet thick, so the place never needed air conditioning in summer and only a small furnace to keep it toasty through the rainy Breton winter.

On the other three sides of the courtyard sat various farm buildings. There was the stone barn where Samuel's grandmother had hand-milked twenty-five cows every morning and afternoon, the big round outdoor bread oven that used to be fired up once a week to bake dozens of loaves at once, the corrugated metal shed that still housed the Fiat tractor and the now-empty henhouse and rabbit cages, and then the enormous pole barn, under which hay and straw were stacked and the family's donkey and multiple cats took refuge whenever the sky opened its vast reservoir.

Stretching out behind all the buildings was a field dotted with enormous old apple trees, under which Samuel's father now let the neighbors graze their cows, since he no longer kept any of his own. Behind the apple trees, the land sloped away slightly, and then farther away it rippled back up into several more hills that looked like the waves of the sea. Standing behind the house looking out over the green hills traced by hedgerows and topped by a faraway town half hidden by the not-yet-lifted fog, I could easily have believed myself in Ireland or Wales.

"That's not far from the truth," Samuel told me. "Brittany is a Celtic country."

"Celtic?" I said, looking at Jeannette to see if she was as confused as I was. "You mean like Loreena McKennitt Celtic? Bagpipe Celtic?"

Samuel nodded. "Brittany means 'Little Britain.' We have lots of bagpipes here."

Now *there* was a sound I had never associated with France.

Samuel's family were very warm hosts, in spite of—or maybe because of—their recent loss of Samuel's mother. On our first evening with them, Samuel and his father and sister took us out to a *crêperie* in the Old Town of Rennes, where half-timbered houses from the Middle Ages still stood around the Place Sainte Anne. "We actually call these crêpes *'galettes',*" explained Samuel's dad. "They're made from buckwheat flour. When I was young, this is what everyone ate every day for lunch. We covered them with eggs, ham, cheese, and washed it all down with hard cider, made from the apples in our backyard."

When it was time for bed that night, Samuel showed Jeannette and me up to his room. "You're giving us your bed?" I asked. "Where are you going to sleep?"

"On a mattress in the loft over the living room."

As I changed into my pajamas, I examined Samuel's bedroom walls, covered in artifacts from his teenage years. Posters of Led Zeppelin and Pink Floyd. Cards from friends urging him to come visit them in China, Mexico, and Brazil. Hand-copied song lyrics and quotes from famous philosophers and artists. Above his bed was a provocative quote from John Lennon.

As I lay there, slowly drifting into sleep amidst Samuel's adolescent world, I felt he had suddenly become much less mysterious.

He was a man with a home, a family, and a childhood. A man with whom I was starting to feel safe.

The next morning, Samuel showed me a photo album of places he'd visited in Canada. In many of the pictures, he was in the company of a beautiful, blond-haired woman. "Is that Catherine?" I asked.

"Yes," he said, surprised. "How do you know her name?"

"From an email you sent once."

"Well, it's over with her now," he said.

Over the next two days, Samuel took Jeannette and me to see the sites of eastern Brittany: the fortified port city of Saint-Malo and the medieval abbey sitting atop the Mont-Saint-Michel. The drive to and from the Mont-Saint-Michel was an hour and a half each way, and on the trip up, I asked Samuel all about the Mont and the history of Brittany. It turned out that Brittany even had its own language—Breton—akin to Welsh and Cornish. And it was making a comeback in special regional schools the French government had just started allowing.

On the trip back, however, I started running out of conversation topics. Maybe it was all the fresh air, but for whatever reason I found myself making way too many comments about the cows we passed. *"Il y a beaucoup de vaches ici."* (There are lots of cows here.) *"Qu'est-ce qu'elles sont belles!"* (They're so pretty!) *"On n'a pas ce genre de vache aux Etats-Unis."* (We don't have that kind of cow in the States.) I wanted to zap myself with a cattle prod even as the words were coming out of my mouth. I was sure Samuel was inwardly rolling his eyes. If he and I had had an easy, casual friendship for four years, clearly it was only because we hardly saw each other and didn't have a chance to see how little we really had to talk about! By the time Jeannette and I boarded the train back to Paris, I was sure that, as much as I was starting to appreciate his company, Samuel and I would never be more than friends, and probably not very close ones at that.

Besides visiting Brittany and sightseeing in Paris with Jeannette, I spent several days on my own in Paris. Wandering in and out of museums and bookstores. Sitting in cafés writing in a new leather-bound diary. Dreaming about what it would be like to belong in a place like this.

There was one particular day when I sat sipping soup inside a bustling Pain Quotidien restaurant as snow fell on the street outside. I felt a strange energy, of a kind I hadn't known since my days in Nancy. I knew at that moment that I had to come back to France, and for much longer than ten days.

When I got back to New York, I started making inquiries through NYU's French Department, hoping to find some kind of program that would offer me support for going abroad. A few days passed with no response. I started to think the idea of getting support from NYU might be dead in the water. But then, while I was still waiting for a response from the French department, I had an unrelated meeting with a professor in my own field, who happened to notice that I was reading the philosopher Merleau-Ponty in the original French. "Do you speak French?" she asked. "You wouldn't be interested in studying in Paris, would you? The philosophy department's been trying to start an exchange program with the Ecole Normale Supérieure, but so far we can't find anyone who wants to go."

Come again?

That's how, the following fall, I found myself living rent-free at one of the most prestigious graduate schools in Paris. And funnily enough, by that time, Samuel was living in Paris as well.

Samuel had asked me to email him when I arrived in the city, but with my bovine monologue still fresh in my mind, I hesitated. I didn't want him to feel obligated to hang out with me just because he was the only person I knew in Paris. But when I didn't write to him for a few weeks, he ended up emailing me. "Are you in Paris yet?" he asked. "Do you want to have dinner?"

He let me choose the place. And because I was vegan at the time, I settled on a Buddhist vegan restaurant I'd heard good things about. It just happened to be called "La Victoire Suprême du Coeur." The Supreme Victory of the Heart.

"How is NYU?" Samuel asked, as soon as we were seated at our table in the middle of the sleek white dining room.

I told him the name of one of the bigwigs who'd agreed to be on my dissertation committee.

"*Mais c'est une chance énorme!*" Samuel exclaimed. "You are so lucky! You have to take full advantage of this opportunity. You have the possibility of a really brilliant philosophical career."

"I'm just hoping my interest in philosophy holds out long enough for me to finish my dissertation," I confessed. I told Samuel how I was already feeling the urge to start some other, unrelated writing project—something more emotionally engaging. I was thinking about writing a book on the power of speech: on why telling other people our hopes, dreams, and fears is so important to us. Or maybe a screenplay about a woman disguising herself as a man in order to momentarily lift the weight of the world's sexual expectations. Or something on the phenomenology of meaning.

"Have you ever read Nancy Huston?" asked Samuel.

I hadn't.

"You remind me of her," he said. "She grew up in English-speaking Canada but moved to Paris to study linguistics and semiotics at the Sorbonne and never left. You're becoming a true Frenchwoman, just like her. Plus you're a writer." Samuel told me he'd just finished reading a collection of Huston's essays that was out in pocket edition: *Professeurs de désespoir*. Professors of Despair. "She criticizes the way intellectuals take nihilism to be a sign of depth."

It took me about ten seconds that night to realize that, if Samuel and I had been hard up for conversation during our last visit, it wasn't because we had nothing to talk about. It was because Jeannette had been with us, and we had had to limit ourselves to small talk. Or at least to things that Samuel was capable of discussing in English or Jeannette was capable of understanding in French. Now that it was just the two of us and we could converse freely, there was no shutting us up. In fact, it seemed to me like there might be a little flirtation going on. We kept taking turns leaning toward the center of the glass-topped table and smiling.

The next day, I went to the bookstore and bought *Professeurs de désespoir*. Since my arrival in France, I had made a deal with myself. If I got up at 8am and worked on my dissertation until lunchtime, I would let myself have the rest of the day to do whatever I wanted. Usually, this meant browsing the six stories of Gibert Joseph, a monumental bookstore on the Boulevard Saint-Michel. Then settling into a café to read and write for the remainder of the afternoon. So, the day after my dinner with Samuel, I bought a copy of *Professeurs de désespoir* at Gibert Joseph and nestled myself into a booth at Le Luco, home of my favorite *café allongé* and a dangerously luscious *moelleux au chocolat*.

Huston's book described how similarities in the lives of nihilism's greatest icons—who were almost exclusively men and tended to live reclusive lives supported by the domestic labor of female relatives—could be interpreted as causing their conviction that existence was ultimately meaningless. She argued that their visions of the world were inevitably influenced by their lack of enduring, intimate relationships with others, and that there was no reason to give their perspective particular weight in intellectual discussion. In fact, there were many obvious reasons not to.

Huston's essays articulated a frustration I'd been feeling since my arrival in New York three years earlier, when I'd first been exposed to the intellectual world outside Christianity. The nihilistic side of that world really bothered me, especially the way I saw it portrayed in movies like the French film *The Dreamers* or the German film *The Elementary Particles*. But I had trouble figuring out exactly what it was I disliked about it. It was while reading Nancy Huston that the answer came to me. It wasn't that I begrudged artists their portrayals of sadness, suffering, or even despair. Rather, I felt that their portrayals of these feelings were not *tragic* enough, because they portrayed the shadowy side of life without any light to compare it to, without any demonstration of the goodness that was missing.

Samuel had asked me to let him know what I thought of Huston's book if I read it. So I wrote him a long email using my favorite film, *Out of Africa*, as an illustration of the kind of tragedy I identified with. I explained that the beauty of Karen Blixen's farm in Kenya, her relationships with her African workers and friends, and her love affair with Denys Finch Hatton made the audience feel all the more acutely the pain and incomprehensibility of her losing it all. On the other hand, pain portrayed without any contrasting joy seemed to me naïve, superficial, and flat.

Samuel replied asking me to meet him for coffee. "So we can talk more about *Out of Africa*," he said.

The following Friday, Samuel met me on the steps of the Opéra Garnier and showed me to a Starbucks nearby. He'd told me he wanted me to see this particular Starbucks, and I immediately saw why. It was in a converted opera building, and the inside reminded me of the photo of a gilded Viennese café I'd seen a couple of years ago in a Chinese magazine. I'd taken a trip to China because I had a friend who was teaching English there, and because I wanted to check out the country where, as a child, I'd thought God was calling me to be a missionary. I'd spent the fifth through twelfth grades studying Mandarin Chinese, with dreams of the sort of third-world adventures I eventually encountered on my trip: using squatty potties in third-class trains and going a week between showers because the unheated guest house we were staying in had an indoor high of fifty degrees Fahrenheit. And yet my visit to China left me surprisingly unmoved. On a plane flying from Xi'an to Chengdu, I thumbed through the travel magazine I found in the seat pocket in front of me and came upon a small, inset photo of a Viennese waiter bending over a table spread with espresso and croissants. "You don't belong in China," that gleaming photo whispered. "You belong in Europe."

That statement now seemed confirmed, as Samuel and I sat in plush armchairs on either side of a polished wooden coffee table and sipped *café au lait* while discussing *Out of Africa* and relationships between men and women.

I'd spent a fair amount of time that fall thinking about men. I had actually begun worrying that my romantic relationships were getting less serious as time went on. After all, Daniel was my first boyfriend, and I'd dated him for two years and was engaged to him by the end. The next two guys I dated, in New York, I saw for only two months apiece. Then in Paris I went out with a guy who pretty obviously wanted nothing but sex. After a week, I told him that wasn't going to happen, and he immediately buttoned up and left. While I was proud of myself for saying no, I was seriously starting to wonder where I was headed.

I wanted to find someone I could genuinely and lastingly connect with, but I didn't seem to have any good candidates. Every man I thought about, whether from Paris or home, had some aspect of his personality that gave me pause. With the one, it was that he only wanted sex. With another, it was his religious and social conservatism. A third was simply too young. But after receiving Samuel's invitation to coffee, I seriously considered for the first time the prospect of dating *him*. And I surprised myself with a feeling of unqualified rightness.

It helped that I was now a few years older than when he'd visited me in New York. And slightly more experienced. I'd let a guy take my shirt off, if not yet my pants. Dating the fellow who only wanted sex did have the benefit of demonstrating to me that I was able to draw a line when I wanted. It helped, too, that I knew Samuel better than I had three years previously. I had met his family and slept in his childhood bed. And I knew that, if Samuel began to show an interest in dating me now, it would be because of everything he knew about me, not because I was the easiest person to get between the sheets. In fact, the slow, natural development of our friendship, and of any romantic feelings that might now come to light, fit a romantic ideal that I had held for a long time: that of a long friendship followed by a period of charming uncertainty about the other person's level of interest. If once I had felt afraid of what might happen if I showed more than friendly affection toward Samuel, now the thought of dating him filled me with a deep sense of security.

While Samuel and I sipped our coffee and talked abstractly about gender relations, I found myself unconsciously imitating his posture. I leaned forward when he leaned forward, sat back when he sat back. Wasn't that supposed to be a sign of chemistry? We talked for three hours and it felt like twenty minutes.

Eventually, Samuel said he had to leave to catch a train home to Brittany for the weekend. "The apple harvest is next Saturday," he said, as we parted outside Starbucks. "It would be a great opportunity for you to meet more French people. Would you like to come?"

"I'd love to," I said, and kissed him goodbye on both cheeks.

On my walk home, I thought about all the signs I had of Samuel's interest in me: inviting me out to dinner, inviting me for coffee, inviting me to the apple harvest. It seemed like he was probably interested in something more than friendship, but I wasn't absolutely certain. I'd made the mistake before of interpreting enthusiastic friendship as romantic interest. Once, after hanging out for months with a guy in my philosophy program at NYU, I'd finally concluded he was interested in me, only to then glimpse a hickey on his neck, one that I was most definitely not responsible for.

Could it be that Samuel was just very friendly? *Oh, please let him be interested in me*, I thought. *Please let him be as interested in me as I am in him.*

And then I remembered. What Samuel had said three years before, in New York. If we were living in the same place, would I "accept" him as a boyfriend? That was not a question you'd ask of someone you had no romantic interest in! What was I worried about? Samuel had practically asked me out already. The only hitch was that I'd said no. And that was something I could easily rectify.

Back in my room at the ENS, I composed an email that was short and to the point. Or so I thought.

"Hi Samuel," it said. "Thanks so much for this afternoon. I always have a great time hanging out with you. But I have a hard time believing what you say about the faults of the French." (That afternoon, Samuel had told me that one of the great downfalls of French people was that they were always comparing themselves to each other. "*Et ils sont tellement conformistes!* They get indignant about anybody who tries to be the slightest bit different!") "I have a hard time believing that the French are as bad as all that," I said, "when I'm sitting across from someone as intelligent and kind as you."

Writing those words felt audacious. Like I was throwing caution to the wind. I felt there was no way Samuel could mistake my meaning. And, in fact, I was so sure that my email would end with me in Samuel's arms at the apple harvest that, once I had written it, I couldn't sit still. It was past ten o'clock at night, but I went out to walk the streets of

Paris: past the Palais du Luxembourg and Saint-Sulpice, down toward Saint-Germain-des-Prés.

Somewhere in the Rue Mabillon, I passed a store window displaying strollers. I paused and looked at them in the light of the streetlamps and suddenly had a vision of myself pushing one of them down a sidewalk, with Samuel at my elbow. I realized that, if given the chance, I would sleep with Samuel. That was how much I trusted him. I felt entirely comfortable at the idea of displaying to him my sexual naïveté. And I also felt certain that, if worst came to worst and I got pregnant, Samuel would do everything in his power to take care of me.

Suddenly, I could very clearly see myself living in France—making a life in France with Samuel—and being wildly happy. Of course, I knew he'd said he didn't want to get married, and that might mean he didn't want to have children either. But that didn't bother me anymore. I was prepared to liberalize my values for him. I was prepared not to have children. Or to have children without being married. To live like so many modern French couples: utterly devoted to one another without the need for a ring. All I needed, I realized, was the love of the man I'd spent my whole life waiting for. The man I trusted entirely and completely.

Chapter
FOUR

The week leading up to the apple harvest seemed interminable. Like waiting for Christmas when you're five years old. Samuel had reserved us a couple of spots with a Paris-Rennes carpooling service, and all I could think about was the fact that, on Friday night, the two of us would be spending four hours sitting in the dark in the back seat of a car.

I was too excited to focus on my dissertation, or any of my other usual occupations. Thursday afternoon, the only activity that could hold my attention was shopping for clothes—something that under normal circumstances I would have judged unbearable. But it would be cold when we collected the apples, so I needed a sweater. And not just any sweater. Something that would make me look irresistibly sexy.

After searching almost every store in the *centre commercial* at Place d'Italie, I finally found what I was looking for: a chocolate-colored pullover, thick but fitted, with a coquettish little hood.

After that, I turned to Gibert Joseph. I bought Nancy Huston's most recent novel, *Lignes de faille*, which came highly recommended by Samuel, and I settled into the nearby Café Luxembourg to read. The opening chapter, I discovered, was written from the perspective of a six-year-old boy who was convinced he was God. I laughed out loud in the café, delighted that Samuel had appreciated this book and wondering if it was because he saw anything of himself in this kid.

Finally, the big day dawned. I spent the whole morning on a leisurely walk to the famous *pâtisserie* Ladurée to buy macaroons for Samuel's family. The kind that were made of two little wafers sealed together by jelly or cream and that came in dozens of tempting flavors, like *pistache* and *chocolat pure origine Venezuela*. I spent the afternoon getting dressed: shaving my legs, choosing my shoes, putting my hair up, taking my hair down, putting my hair up again.

The driver had told us to meet her at five in front of the mall at Porte d'Italie. I double-checked the email, because there were two metro stops in Paris that had "Italie" in the name: *Porte* d'Italie and *Place* d'Italie. I knew there was a mall at the latter, because that's where I'd bought my sweater. But the email clearly said *Porte* d'Italie. So I showed up at Porte d'Italie at five o'clock, with my fancy green and white bag of macaroons over my arm. I emerged from the metro and did several rounds of the intersection, looking up and down the avenues. There were a lot of apartment buildings and some bars, but no mall in sight. I walked a few hundred yards each way on the Avenue d'Italie as well as on its cross street, but still no sign of a mall.

By now it was 5:20, and for the first time, I began to regret my decision not to get a cell phone in France. If I didn't find Samuel and our driver soon, they were going to be forced to leave without me.

Doing my best to remain calm, I walked around the Porte d'Italie intersection for the seventh time. On each round, a young woman had tried to hand me a flyer about a buy-one-get-one-free sale on shoes. Finally, I took it from her. I tried to smile, but there were tears in my eyes. The look she gave me in return was so sympathetic that it stopped me in my tracks. "*Excusez-moi de vous déranger*," I said. "But could I borrow your cell phone? I was supposed to meet someone here, and I can't find them anywhere, and it's twenty-five minutes past—"

"*Tenez*," she said, handing me her phone.

Thankfully, I had written Samuel's number on a tiny slip of paper tucked inside my wallet. He picked up right away. "*Allô, oui?*"

"*C'est Sharon*," I said. "Have you left yet?"

"No—where are you?"

"At Porte d'Italie. Where you said to meet."

"I'm sorry," he said. "We're at *Place* d'Italie, not Porte. I realized at the last minute that's what she must have meant. There's no mall at Porte d'Italie."

"Yeah, I know."

"I'm sorry. I figured it out too late to write and tell you."

"What should we do?" I asked.

"We'll wait for you, *bien sûr*."

I ran back into the metro, onto an extraordinarily crowded platform. Place d'Italie was only two stops away. It wouldn't take more than five minutes to join them, once the train arrived. But as I stood and waited, I realized there could only be one reason that the platform was so crowded: the trains must have stopped running. A garbled intercom announcement eventually confirmed that they wouldn't be back on line for some time.

So I bolted back up the metro steps, my poor macaroons still in tow. There had to be a bus that went straight down the Avenue d'Italie. I asked the woman with the flyers where to catch it. After wasting a ticket on the metro, I had one last transit ticket in my wallet, and I used it to board the bus. Finally, at 5:50, I jumped out and ran across Place d'Italie to where Samuel and the driver were waiting, directly in front of the mall where I'd bought my sexy sweater.

But there was nothing sexy left about me. When I fell into the back seat of the driver's Peugeot, I was a sweaty, disheveled mess. I peeked into the bag of macaroons and saw that they, too, were but remnants of their formerly enticing selves.

Fortunately, the sun set quickly as we passed out of the suburbs of Paris, disguising my disarray and leaving Samuel and me in a very intimate state of darkness, lit only by the headlights of cars passing on the highway. I had planned to find a way to cozy up to him—maybe to feign sleepiness and lay my head on his shoulder the way I'd once done with Daniel on a long car ride to the Jersey shore. But Samuel had too much to say. "What do you think of the scandal at your school?" he asked. "It's all over the papers that the *directrice* of the ENS wants to make alumni pay for library access."

Leave it to the French to make library fees a national scandal! "Well," I said. "If the government won't give them enough money to run the library any other way.... There's definitely not a surplus of funds at the ENS." Frankly, I'd been a little shocked at the state of the classrooms and dormitories at a school renowned as one of the best in France. After all, Sartre and de Beauvoir had studied there. I'd figured it would be state-of-the-art. But, instead, the school appeared to still be hanging on to the same tables and chairs that had graced those halls in the days of Sartre and de Beauvoir. And I was pretty sure that was the last time the bathrooms had been cleaned.

"Have you met the *directrice*?" asked Samuel. "Did you know she was friends with Nancy Huston in school? She's married to an American philosopher."

The entire car ride was filled with talk of the ENS, philosophy, and politics. When we reached Rennes around 10pm, we were both still wide awake, and my head hadn't come within eighteen inches of Samuel's shoulder. I found myself wishing for the days when it seemed like Samuel and I had nothing to say to one another.

We were met in Rennes by Samuel's father and sister, who took us home and fed us a potato casserole, then graciously sampled my macaroon crumbs. After dinner, Samuel told me he wanted to lend me a philosophy book. "That book by Michael Dummett I was telling you about," he said. "It's in my room."

As he searched his shelves, I lay on his bed. Propping myself up with one arm and looking as inviting as I dared. I thought I saw him glance at me out of the corner of his eye, but then he plunked Michael Dummett's *Truth and Other Enigmas* in my hand. "Want to help me make the *vin chaud*?" he asked, and headed for the door.

We went back downstairs to prepare an enormous pot of mulled wine for the next day. And once it was simmering on the stove, we went to bed: I in his room, he next door in the loft.

The next morning dawned frosty and foggy. We were going to start work early so all the apples would be in the trailer by noon, when we'd break out the meal, mulled wine, and music. I came downstairs in my sexy new sweater, and Samuel immediately exclaimed, "You're going to be cold in that! Let me get you a coat." He handed me a shapeless quilted jacket three sizes too big.

But no one in the group of thirty-odd helpers was looking too stylish in their work coats, wool hats, and huge rubber boots—useful for walking through the tall, wet grass of the orchard. The cows hadn't been allowed in to pasture there for a while, because they would have eaten all the fallen apples, and the fallen apples were what we were after. For selling to a cider house.

We all waded around in the wet grass for a while, slowly progressing across the orchard, taking breaks here and there to warm our hands and have some coffee from the thermos kept hot on the engine of the tractor. Finally, our sweep of the area was complete, and we could permanently straighten our backs and head for the barn where Samuel's aunt and cousins had the food waiting. There were two great pots of soup and all manner of side dishes that had been baking all morning in the outdoor oven. Samuel's grandmother had made her famous rabbit pâté, and there was the mulled wine and the obligatory trays of baked cinnamon apples, so we could taste some of the fruits of our labor.

Once everyone was reenergized by the food, the music began. Everyone, it seemed, had brought an instrument. There were accordions, flutes, a pennywhistle, and—true to Samuel's word—bagpipes. Samuel brought out a guitar. I happily spent the majority of the afternoon listening to him strum and pick, and joining in the singing whenever there was a rare song I knew.

When the sun began to go down, the people who hadn't yet gone home crowded into the farmhouse kitchen for a cup of tea. I saw Samuel slip out to the living room, and a few minutes later, I followed him. He was building a fire, while a two-year-old girl stood by fiddling with some sticks from the woodpile. I played with her for a while, happy to have an excuse for staying near Samuel. "Did you have fun?" he asked me.

"It was wonderful. Thanks so much for inviting me."

"Of course."

When the fire started crackling, Samuel returned to the kitchen.

After all the guests had finally gone home, Samuel and his father and sister and I shared a late supper of cheese and smoked ham. The atmosphere around the kitchen table was warm and comfortable, like being home for the Christmas holidays. We lingered after the meal, and Samuel brought out a bottle of Scotch, which he poured into glasses for himself and his father. "Could I try some?" I asked.

Samuel looked at me in surprise. "Really?"

"*Oui*...."

"Well, good! I'm glad!" he said. He got up to get another glass, and rested his hand very briefly on my forearm.

Around 1am, we finally got up from the table. "Do you want to sing some more?" Samuel asked me. "We could try a song from the new Coldplay album. The hidden track." He got us some stools so we could sit in front of the living room stereo while he played his guitar along with the CD. He had a lead sheet, and I sang along, improvising a second melody in the space between the lyrics to "'Til Kingdom Come." Why had he chosen this song in particular? I wondered. The lyrics were all about having waited many long years for someone—someone who held the keys to unlock the singer's heart—and about being willing to wait many more years for this person, if need be. 'Til Kingdom Come.

"*C'est génial!*" Samuel exclaimed, when the song was over. "You have such a beautiful voice, Sharon. Papa! Gwendoline! Come in here and listen to Sharon sing this song!"

We did the whole song again for his sister and dad, including the ending in which Chris Martin implores the listener six times over to *please wait for him, too*. I couldn't help wondering whether Samuel was thinking about what we were singing. Were these lyrics resonating as deeply with him as they were with me?

"All right," said Samuel's dad at the close of the song. "Time to go to bed. Put the guitar away."

"Just a few more," said Samuel, pulling out sheets for a couple of U2 songs.

After another ten minutes or so, his dad and sister went up to their rooms, and Samuel turned to me. "We really should stop. But let's do 'Kingdom Come' one more time."

He started the CD again, and I again sang the lyrics that seemed so close to describing our own situation. Someone knocking at the door asking to be allowed in. Waiting for years upon years for a moment of divine fulfillment.

When Samuel finally put his guitar away, I went into the kitchen to get a glass of water, purposely lingering at the sink to see whether he might want to stay up and talk, just the two of us. I wanted tonight to be the opposite of that night in New York when I'd run away at the end of *Romeo + Juliet*. But when Samuel finally popped his head in the kitchen, all he said was, "*Bonne nuit.*" And then he went up to bed.

The next day, we went back to Paris: Samuel, his sister, and me. Samuel drove one of his dad's cars, and he and his sister spent most of the trip in a very animated conversation that I had no hope of joining, especially from the backseat. So I listened to the radio. There was a song on about "*les bobos.*"

"Who's this?" I asked, leaning forward so they could hear me. "Is he talking about *bourgeois bohémiens*?"

"*Oui. C'est Renaud.* Do you know him?"

"Did Renaud get the idea from David Brooks' book *Bobos in Paradise*, or the other way around?" I asked.

"*Je sais pas,*" said Samuel.

It was the only half-intelligent thing I said the whole car ride, but it didn't make much of an impression on the conversation. Samuel and his sister went back to talking, and I went back to staring out the window. Despite all my dreaming and hoping and utter certainty that Samuel was interested in me, the verdict of the weekend appeared once again to be that he would never be more than a friend.

Just to be sure, after I got back to my dorm at the ENS, I sent him an email inviting him to celebrate Thanksgiving with me and my American friends that coming Thursday. But the day came and went with no reply from Samuel. The next day, I took an overnight train to Berlin, to spend a couple of weeks sightseeing in Germany and Austria. I put Samuel out of my mind and focused instead on enjoying Germany's Christmas markets, complete with *Glühwein* and some addictive cinnamon pastries.

About a week into the trip, while I was at a hostel in Freiberg, I got an email from Samuel. He said he was sorry he'd missed Thanksgiving, but he'd had to make an unexpected trip back to Brittany. As though to make up for it, he mentioned that his uncle worked at the Comédie Française, Paris's most prestigious theater, and had offered to give us a tour. "Would you be available next Friday?" he asked. Samuel also mentioned that he had a friend who'd be defending his dissertation at the Université de Rennes that same weekend. "There'll be a big party afterward," he said. "Do you want to go? We could stay at my dad's afterward."

All I could think was, could Samuel *really* be oblivious to the implications of inviting a woman to stay with his family twice in one month? I didn't think so, but then again, he'd surprised me before. And I wasn't really a party kind of girl. I'd be disappointed if this weekend turned out just like the apple harvest, with Samuel's attention directed to everyone but me. I decided to mull things over for a day or two.

Meanwhile, I continued on to Vienna. And came down with food poisoning my first night in town. Apparently, my traveling buddy didn't see the harm in straining your pasta with a dirty towel you found wadded up on the kitchen counter of a hostel. I spent the duration of our visit to Vienna in bed, unable to eat…or do anything else besides make frequent trips to the toilet.

By the night I was supposed to take the train back to Paris, I felt just well enough to make it from the hostel to the train station without doubling over. It was then that I realized I'd never responded to Samuel's invitation. It was Wednesday night, and he'd asked me to visit the Comédie Française that Friday morning and go to Brittany Friday evening. I wasn't entirely convinced I was going to make it back to Paris alive, but I forced my aching body into an internet café. In what I hoped was comprehensible French, I told Samuel I was finally starting to recover from being very sick and that I thought it would be better for me to stay in Paris that weekend to recuperate. On the other hand, I would be glad to join him and his uncle at the Comédie Française on Friday.

That taken care of, I boarded the train, stretched out on my bunk, and promptly lost consciousness. I awoke only once before Paris—when the train made a brief stop in Nancy. I heard the unmistakable chime of the French railway system, and I knew deep in my bones that everything was going to be all right.

In fact, when I arrived in Paris Thursday morning, I felt immediately better. I was still weak from having eaten nothing but three pudding cups in three days (oh, and one ill-advised piece of Viennese cheese toast!), but my appetite was back. For the next week, I bought *pains au chocolat* two at a time and devoured them before I was even a block from the *boulangerie*.

Paris looked even better than when I'd left, everything bright and crisp in the late autumn sunshine. After Friday's backstage tour of the Comédie Française, I sipped an espresso with Samuel and his uncle while we waited for a sudden rainstorm to clear up. Then I kissed them both goodbye, telling Samuel I would see him when I got back from Christmas break. As I walked up the Avenue de l'Opéra, the clouds were just beginning to part, and in the few rays of sun that made their way through, I caught a glimpse of something magical: the first snowflakes of the season, floating lazily to the ground.

Back home in Virginia, I listened to a CD I'd bought: Renaud singing about *les bobos*. It made me think about Samuel. Made me wonder again whether his second invitation to spend a weekend in Brittany had been a sign of the potential for something more. Maybe it had. But I realized that, even if Samuel had previously been thinking along those lines, he'd probably ruled out the possibility by now. He knew that, after Christmas, I'd only be returning to Paris for one more month. Hardly enough time to start a transatlantic romance.

But then, a few days before Christmas, I got a surprise email from the Ecole Normale Supérieure. "The NYU student who was intending to take your place for the spring semester has elected not to come to Paris after all," wrote the administrator. "You are thus welcome to stay on at the ENS through June." Was there any other philosophy department in the world, I wondered, where people were so reluctant to take a free room in Paris? But I couldn't complain. After getting the okay from my dissertation advisors, the first person I told was Samuel. "I'm staying in France for the spring!" I gleefully typed.

"Good news!" he replied.

When I got back to Paris in early January, Samuel immediately invited me out to dinner. He chose the place this time: a Lebanese restaurant in the 9th arrondissement. Near his apartment. After we'd studied the menu and placed our orders, he handed me a package wrapped in red paper. "A belated Christmas present," he said.

I unwrapped it to reveal a book by someone named Tzvetan Todorov.

"It just came out," said Samuel. "It's by Nancy Huston's husband."

"Wow." It was such a thoughtful, personal gift. I looked him in the eye as I thanked him. "This is really wonderful. *Merci.*"

Samuel and I spent the meal discussing what we'd done over the holidays, as well as all the recent developments in French politics—developments that were growing ever more important as the presidential elections approached in May. When we left the restaurant, we walked slowly towards the metro. "Do you feel like doing anything else?" Samuel asked.

"Sure," I said, glancing up at the surrounding apartment buildings and wondering if one of them might be his. I had read in a foreigner's guide to France that, if a Frenchman invites you up to his apartment and you accept, you've both tacitly agreed to end up in bed. And by this point, I felt more than ready to love Samuel, fully and without reserve.

But that was apparently not what he had in mind. "I've been wanting to try this bar at the end of the street," he said. And so we ordered a couple of cognacs and talked for another hour amid a sea of empty tables.

It was early March before I saw Samuel again. We met in République one afternoon for coffee, so I could get back a book I'd loaned him. I showed him the latest Nancy Huston I'd been reading. And, with the hope of making him just the slightest bit jealous, I worked into our conversation an anecdote about a guy I'd met on a recent weekend while out swing dancing. When we parted at the metro, I told Samuel I was going back to the States for a couple of weeks at the end of the month and hoped he'd suggest doing something again before then. But all he said was, "Let me know when you get back."

When I did get back, in April, I invited him out with me and my friend Alexandra to hear some jazz. But, on the appointed evening, Alexandra's cell phone suddenly died, and I couldn't get ahold of Samuel to tell him the address of the club. Even my prepaid card for the pay phone had mysteriously lost all its minutes. "They expire," said Alexandra, matter-of-factly. So I walked fifteen minutes back to the

ENS to send Samuel an email, but he still didn't get it in time to meet us.

That was the evening on which I finally gave up. As much as I liked Samuel, and as much chemistry as we had had back in the fall, it seemed that our stars were simply not aligned. Any more wishing seemed like a waste of energy.

So I continued to spend my days in Paris as I always had: working on my dissertation in the morning, browsing the shelves at Gibert Joseph in the early afternoon, then reading or writing as the mood struck. The weather began to warm up, and I exchanged my cafés for the banks of the Seine, the benches of the Jardin des Plantes, and the outdoor tea room at the nearby mosque, where the scent of mint filled the air and sparrows hopped from table to table searching for pastry crumbs. On those long, reflection-filled afternoons, I thought a lot about men, but no longer about Samuel.

Then, at the end of April, three weeks before I would be leaving Paris for good, Samuel sent me an email. "Can I take you to dinner next week?" he asked. That was the entire email. Just that one line.

"Sure!" I replied. "How's Thursday?"

The Monday before we were supposed to go out, Samuel wrote me again to say that Ségolène Royal, one of the final two candidates in the upcoming presidential election, was going to be speaking at Charléty Stadium the next afternoon. Did I want to go see her?

As I was heading out the door to meet him, hope again fluttering in my chest, I ran into an American friend of mine, Shira. "Where are you off to?" she asked. Shira was a big fan of Royal, and I knew that if I told her where I was going, she would want to come along. But if there was one part of my conservative Christian upbringing I could never quite shake, it was the inability to lie. "To Charléty to see Ségolène Royal," I confessed.

"Oh! Can I come?"

I wanted so badly to keep Samuel all to myself, to spend a grand afternoon squished up next to him on the bleachers of the Stade Charléty. But, honestly, what reason did I have to expect that there were any romantic possibilities left for us? The probability that anything would come of this outing seemed so low that I would have felt foolish protesting that it was a date. Which meant that, when I emerged from the metro near the stadium, Samuel saw that I had a friend in tow. And if the chance of something's happening between us had been slim before, it now felt like it was officially zero.

"Do you think Samuel still wants to go out to dinner on Thursday?" I asked Shira the next afternoon, in the middle of a class she and I were taking on Arab cooking. "When we got off the metro yesterday, he didn't say, 'See you Thursday.' Do you think going to see Ségolène was supposed to replace the dinner we had planned? We've never hung out twice in one week before."

"*Sharon.*" Shira looked up from the counter where she was carefully forming her pastry dough. "Yesterday, Samuel asked you *three times* what you were doing later."

I realized she was right. I'd been avoiding answering because I wasn't sure if he was asking just me, or me *and* Shira.

"He wants to see you again," Shira reassured me. "Just write him and ask."

So I did. "Do you still want to go out to dinner on Thursday?" I wrote.

Samuel replied within the hour: "*Gardons l'idée.*" Let's keep the idea. Meaning, let's stick to our original plan.

I don't know how I managed once more to rekindle the hope that something would develop between Samuel and me, after all the perfect opportunities we'd already squandered. And especially now that I had only two weeks left in Paris. But Thursday morning, while I worked on revisions to my dissertation, butterflies took up residence in my stomach. And something felt different this time. Something about the way Samuel had worded his invitation. It was so direct: "Can I take you to dinner?" No reason given. Maybe it was a cultural difference, but if I had gotten that email from any of my American guy friends, I would have definitely suspected that something was up.

And yet we still had one more hurdle to overcome. An hour before I planned to leave to meet Samuel, I received a gut-wrenching email from my mother. "I've been putting off saying anything to you about this," she began, "but I can't keep it in anymore. I wake up almost every morning crying uncontrollably, thinking what it would be like to lose you forever." She meant in hell.

My mom had known for a long time that I didn't believe in Jesus anymore. It had been six and a half years since I'd first revealed my religious doubts to my parents, in a phone conversation during my sophomore year of college. That conversation had begun, oddly enough, with my confession that I no longer found myself able to believe in hell. "If eternal life with God is the best, most enjoyable life we can have," I said, "then anyone who doesn't choose it must not *know* how good it is, or they must not have enough willpower. Neither of those things seems like a good reason for God to send someone to hell."

"God is perfectly just," replied my mom. "He would never send anyone to hell if they didn't deserve it."

"Of course not," I said. "I'm not saying he does."

"God isn't like us," interjected my dad. "He's perfectly holy. So holy he can't even look on sin. If someone doesn't repent, God can't let them into his presence."

"But isn't God present here on earth?" I asked. "And isn't God's work to be constantly drawing people to himself? Why wouldn't he keep doing that until everyone was saved?"

"Some people don't want to be saved," said my dad, with genuine sadness in his voice.

"Why wouldn't they?" I countered. "I don't see how anyone could reject God unless they didn't understand what they were doing. And if God can send someone like that to be tortured—for *eternity*—then what does it even mean to call God 'just'? Eternal punishment is infinitely worse than anything Hitler did. If I, as limited in my capacity for love as I am, can't imagine condemning anyone to hell, it makes no sense to say that God is *so* good he can do one of the most heinous things imaginable."

"Are you *judging God*?" asked my mother. There was a clear edge to her voice, but I couldn't tell if it was from anger or fear. "God's ways are much higher than ours, Sharon. The Bible *says* there are people who are knowingly and willingly in rebellion against God, and that God is just to punish them. It's extremely arrogant for you to think you know better than God."

"I'm not *saying* I know better than God," I insisted, tears beginning to fill my eyes. "I'm saying, because I believe God *is* perfectly just and loving, maybe we're wrong to think he sends people to hell. Maybe we've been misinterpreting the Bible."

"Scripture is very clear on this. *Jesus* is very clear on this."

I didn't know how to explain the fact that it wasn't obvious to me anymore that every word of the Bible was divinely inspired. My college Bible classes had exposed me to so many different theories of Biblical inspiration and interpretation, I could no longer take it for granted that God had dictated every book of the Bible word for word. Where was the evidence? How did I know that any particular passage reflected absolute divine truth and wasn't merely the product of an author who wanted others to *believe* his words were divine? Evangelical Christianity said we were not supposed to rely on our own judgment but on the revealed Word of God, but it seemed impossible to avoid using your own judgment. How else could you determine whether something *was* the revealed Word of God? You couldn't just go around believing anyone who said their messages were from God. "I think maybe hell is a human idea," I squeaked out.

"If that's the case," replied my mother, "then why did Jesus have to suffer and die on the cross? Are you saying all of that was unnecessary?"

I bowed my head. It was extremely hard for me to question beliefs that I knew were so dear to my parents. Until then, my allegiance to their religious views had always been absolute. But now that the way in which I saw the world was changing, I needed to share that with my parents. I needed them to understand. And honestly, I was hoping they might be able to change my mind. "I don't know," I confessed.

"It's dangerous not to know," continued my mom. "If you don't believe in hell, if you don't believe there's something you need saving from, then how are you going to be sure to avoid it?"

I answered her with the utmost sincerity. "I believe that, if God exists, God loves me, and he won't condemn me for being unable to see how he could send people to hell."

"*If* God exists? Belief is a choice, Sharon. Your job is to trust that God's ways are higher than yours, that they go far beyond what your human mind can grasp."

The phone conversation had ended with me crumpling to the floor in tears, shattered because I was unable to make my parents see that I was seeking the truth the best way I knew how—that my heart was filled not with intellectual hubris but love, and a desire for a God I could wholeheartedly embrace.

Since that time, I'd come to realize that my mother was not so much angry or disappointed in me as she was deeply worried. I'd seen intermittent signs of her angst over my condition. Mostly in the quiet way in which she every so often gave me books on Christianity to read, books like *Letters to a Skeptic* and *The Divine Conspiracy*. The fewer words my mom used, the more emotional I knew she was. But recently I thought she'd been coming to terms with my new identity. Over Christmas, she and I had had a long conversation about my love life, and when I'd expressed some frustration at my lack of marriage prospects, she'd asked, "What about Samuel?" I was surprised she would even mention him. After all, a few years ago, I'd told my parents that Samuel was living with his girlfriend in Canada, so my mom knew his sexual mores were different from hers. Nevertheless, she now reminded me that, in my Thanksgiving email to my parents, I'd written, "Maybe I could marry a Frenchman after all."

Indeed, I *had* written that, when I realized that Samuel was not like the other Frenchmen I knew—gaunt, bespectacled intellectuals with incurable addictions to black turtlenecks and existential angst. Samuel actually managed a fair amount of enthusiasm for life and other people. And sometimes he even wore pastels.

For my mother to bring Samuel up in the context of a discussion of marriage was highly significant to me. It made me think she was starting to accept that I was different from her and that she wanted my happiness even if it meant being with someone from a very different background. It made me tear up. But now I wondered if that acceptance had all been in my imagination.

The email she sent me about fearing I'd end up in hell made me feel sorry for her, but it also made me resentful. Resentful that she seemed to be blaming me for beliefs I had no power to change. "You have to know that this tears me apart," she wrote, as though I could do something about it. Why was she holding me responsible for her suffering when it seemed like the thing to do was for her to stop believing that her daughter—who by every objective measure had for the past twenty-five years been pursuing truth and goodness to the very best of her ability—was going to hell? At the same time, I supposed she was no more capable of ceasing to believe that than I was capable of returning to belief in the saving power of Jesus. So I replied to her as compassionately as I could, with a promise to sit down and talk about things that summer when I was home.

After that, I didn't feel much like going out. I just wanted to curl up in a ball and cry myself to sleep. I certainly couldn't see myself being a good date. And it hardly seemed worth the effort, given that the outcome of the evening would doubtless be the same as always. But as I slouched at my computer, staring at the clear spring sky stretching out over my balcony, I felt my tears slowly dry and a whisper of motivation return. I found myself slipping on a skirt. And a black sleeveless top with a generous décolleté.

Samuel met me at Métro Abbesses, wearing a black sport coat and holding a newspaper tucked under one arm. We walked to the nearby bar Le Vrai Paris. "Are you okay?" he asked.

I was feeling so much better than an hour previously that I was surprised he'd noticed anything amiss. "Oh, yeah. I'm fine. Just a little tired."

As we sipped our Guinness and discussed the previous night's presidential debate, I gradually began to feel more like myself. I eventually launched into a vehement criticism of Nicolas Sarkozy's debate style. "He treats Royal like a child!" I fumed. "Like he's there to educate her! When the things she's saying are incredibly intelligent, if he'd actually *listen* to any of them."

Samuel and I ordered a second round. And when we'd finished that, he suggested we go next door to eat. By the time we had dinner and a bottle of wine in front of us, I was feeling enough distance from the emotions of the afternoon to mention my mother's email to him. "Why would someone believe something that's so painful for them?" I asked Samuel. "Why would they believe that God would be cruel enough to send someone to hell who just wants to figure out the truth?"

"Your mum doesn't know any other way to believe."

"I just don't understand what she thinks I've been doing. I've been seeking God my whole life. It's not my fault if he hasn't responded! The proof is I keep trying to come back to Christianity. And I always end up friends with people who are very spiritual. Even you. The one non-atheist in France, and I'm your friend!"

Samuel smiled. He took a bite of his entrée and chewed it thoughtfully. "What do you think spirituality *is*?" he eventually asked.

"You know, it's funny, because I've been thinking about that lately," I said. "About what it is that all the people I seem to be attracted to as friends have in common. And I think it has something to do with feeling like you're part of something much bigger than yourself, and feeling a responsibility toward that larger whole. A spiritual person cares a lot about what's good and right. They don't see their life as meaningless, or as just a matter of having fun or being successful. There's a sense of conviction. Even if the content of our convictions is different, at least we *have* some."

It was past midnight when I realized I'd been so engrossed in the conversation that I'd hardly touched my food. The waiters were wiping down tables and straightening chairs. Samuel paid the bill as I ate a few bites of *salade niçoise* and downed some cold fries.

"Do you want to take a walk by Sacré Coeur?" asked Samuel. "There's a statue over there I want to show you."

The night air was still warm, and perfumed by newly opened lilacs. The Sacred Heart basilica was only five minutes away on foot, but when we arrived at the foot of its giant flight of steps, we saw that the lights illuminating the façade had already been turned off. We checked our watches. It was 1am.

"How late does the metro run?" I asked Samuel.

"The last train probably comes around 1:15."

"I should hurry then."

"I'll walk with you," he said. "The closest stop on the 7 is by my apartment."

We walked briskly down the hill from Sacré Coeur, across the Boulevard de Rochechouart, and beside a long park surrounded by a wrought-iron fence. When we were within sight of the metro, Samuel gestured up a narrow street that veered off at a diagonal. "My place is up there. I rent a room from a woman and her son. But I'm thinking of getting my own place soon." I wondered if this was part of why he'd never invited me up.

As we continued a few more steps down toward the station, just to have something to say, I asked, "So you really think you'll be leaving that apartment soon?"

"Maybe," said Samuel. Then he suddenly stopped walking and turned to me. "Would you like to see it?"

"Sure," I said. Very casually. As though we didn't both know that it meant missing the last train.

We walked back up the hill and up Samuel's diagonal street to an enormous green door where he had to punch a code into a brass keypad. Then we tiptoed across the marble floor of the foyer to the elevator, housed in an old-fashioned steel cage. Samuel held the door and motioned me inside.

The elevator was tiny. I could smell Samuel's cologne as we stood almost touching. I looked into the mirror attached to one wall and nervously tapped my thumb on the strap of my purse as the cage jerked into motion. We rose through five awkward floors before the elevator finally opened to a landing with a pair of massive oak doors.

It was late, so the tour Samuel gave me of the apartment was a bit dark—and whispered—but I could immediately see why Samuel had not been too unhappy sharing this place. It was gorgeous, with high ceilings, floor-to-ceiling windows, and exquisite Art Nouveau detailing at every turn. After the common areas, Samuel let me into his room. It, too, had high ceilings, beautiful moldings, and an enormous fireplace. And it was bigger than my entire apartment in Manhattan. There was room for a desk, a big oak table, a massive armoire, a dresser, a weight machine off in the back corner, and a king-size bed. And every surface—save a square meter or so of the bed—was covered in books.

"Would you like some wine?" asked Samuel, pulling a bottle off the mantle. He poured us each a glass of red. "Should I put on some music?"

He shuffled through some CD cases that were sitting on his mini-fridge, then popped one into the player. It was Aretha Franklin singing love ballads, starting with "What a Difference a Day Makes."

We clinked glasses and each took a sip of wine. I let my eyes wander across the room to the bed. So this was where Samuel slept. Every night when we'd parted, this is what he'd come home to. He'd lay here, his head on one of these very pillows. I looked shyly at him. He took another sip of wine and moved a step toward me.

Then he passed me and went to his desk, where he sat down and opened his laptop.

I wasn't sure what to make of this development, so I followed him. I sat down on the edge of the bed next to the desk and acted as though browsing the internet was the obvious next step after wine and romantic music. Samuel looked up my profile on the NYU website. Then he checked the news. Then he pulled up some information on a Breton electric guitarist. "Do you know Gildas Arzel?" he asked. "I have one of his albums around here somewhere."

He got up and started going through his stacks of CDs again. "You should know this, too," he said. "Natasha St. Pier. And Johnny Hallyday. You do know Johnny Hallyday, don't you?"

"Just by name."

Samuel sat back down at his desk to sort the discs. Finally, he collected eight or nine of them into a pile. "You can take these if you want," he said, handing them to me.

This seemed strangely like a cue to leave. I held the CDs in mid-air for a moment, mentally reviewing the events of the last thirty-odd minutes. Was it possible I could have been totally, brutally mistaken about the meaning of being invited up to his apartment?

Samuel must have seen the confusion on my face at that moment. And it must have given him some information he'd been waiting for, because he immediately took the CDs back and laid them on the desk.

"*Mais je te garde ce soir,*" he said. But I'm keeping you tonight.

He leaned gently toward me, I leaned gently toward him, and our lips finally met with a sweetness only five years and seven months of suspense could have produced.

Chapter
FIVE

The first months that Samuel and I spent together felt surreal. It was so strange to think that the man I now knew so intimately was the same man I'd been scared of back in New York in October 2003. The man I'd had trouble making conversation with in January 2006. The man who, for the last seven months, had seemed always on the verge of a romantic gesture and yet had never made a definitive move. "I can't believe nothing happened that weekend I came to Brittany for the apple harvest," I told Samuel soon after we started dating.

"I didn't know you were interested," he said.

"But I specifically wrote you that email. The one where I said how intelligent and charming you were and how I loved hanging out with you."

"I thought you were brushing me off. Like you were saying, 'You're really nice and everything, but....'"

"Seriously? I thought I was being so over-the-top obvious! I was *so* interested in you."

"I do remember you sitting on my bed that night, when I was looking for the book. You looked...sexier."

"See? You *did* know I was interested!"

"But then I invited you to Brittany again, and you didn't come."

"Because I had *food poisoning*. I was deathly ill!"

"I thought it was an excuse."

The surreal feeling bonded us to one another. Our love was the fulfillment of something that had been growing for so many years that there was no doubt in either of our minds that we had been meant to find each other. Finally.

And yet, just three short years later, here I was lying alone in my childhood bedroom, surrounded by boxes full of our dismantled Boston apartment, and there was a new and different surreal quality in our relationship. The man I'd entrusted with my heart and soul had just told me there was another woman in his life.

I woke up repeatedly throughout that night. When I would first open my eyes, I had no memory of anything's being wrong. I'd pull the quilt up around my chin and be about to drift contentedly back to sleep when I would remember with a start, *There is a girl*. My chest would tighten, my breathing would turn shallow, and I would be newly staggered by the realization that this had become my life. How in the world had this sort of searing pain found its way into such a caring, trusting relationship?

Before this, the only time I'd ever gotten close to being jealous of another woman was in a dream—that dream where Samuel's ex-girlfriend showed up at our house with a two-year-old boy she said was his son. I wasn't worried in the dream that Samuel would go back to her. I knew how rocky his relationship with Catherine had been. I knew how relieved he had been to find *me*, someone who didn't berate him for spending hours at his computer writing. Someone who knew how to control her temper. Someone who didn't need to know where he was every hour of the day or night. But in the dream, I was jealous that Catherine had his child. Jealous that she had found a way to insert herself into such an intimate, permanent corner of his life. And, above all, jealous that I would never be the first one to give him a baby.

I had told Samuel about the dream the morning after I had it. He didn't say much at the time. But a couple weeks later he asked me if I'd been secretly reading his email.

"No," I said, a little offended. "I'd never even think of doing that. Why?"

"You told me you had that dream about Catherine having a baby. That was right after she wrote to tell me she was pregnant."

"She's pregnant? Wow." I had heard about people having premonitions in dreams, but this was the first time I could remember anything like that happening to me. "I absolutely did not read your email," I reassured Samuel. "I would never do that without your permission."

"Well, Catherine used to."

"I am very different from Catherine," I said, very pointedly.

It didn't occur to me at the time to wonder why Samuel hadn't told me earlier about Catherine's email. Or to wonder how many other emails he'd gotten from her while we were together. Or whether he was getting emails from anyone else—maybe someone he'd never even mentioned to me? I had trusted him completely without even thinking about it.

And in fact, I still did. Even if Samuel had neglected to tell me that he was going to be seeing one of his old high-school friends the day after I went back to the States for my marriage visa, I genuinely believed that it had only been in an effort not to worry me. He had expected to see this girl one last time and that be that. No need to make me anxious or provoke a lot of questions. He hadn't known what was actually going to happen. No, Samuel was a good man. I firmly believed that. Everything we'd ever lived together proved it.

Three years ago, after our long-awaited first kiss, I had had to tell Samuel that I was still a virgin and wasn't quite ready to sleep with him. "I'm sorry," I said, thinking maybe I'd led him on and he would be resentful.

"You have nothing to be sorry about," Samuel insisted. And the kisses he lavished on my body seemed proof that he harbored no resentment. Only hope for things to come. I fell asleep that night wrapped snugly in his arms.

The next morning was a Friday and Samuel had to go to work, but he called in to say he'd be a couple of hours late. He walked me down a foggy cobblestone street to a little café where he bought us croissants and coffee. We had breakfast together looking out at the gray Parisian sidewalk. "*Merde!*" he suddenly exclaimed.

"What is it?"

"I just remembered I have to go to Brittany this afternoon. For the election." He was registered to vote that weekend in his hometown. French elections were always on Sundays. "What are you doing Monday?" he asked. "I could take the day off, and we could go up the tower at Sacré Coeur."

The fact that he was making plans to see me as soon as he got back into town filled me with warmth. This was not going to be a relationship like any of my others, where I was perpetually left wondering whether the guy really cared for me or not. Our period of ambiguity appeared to be solidly behind us. "That would be great," I said.

When I got back to my room at school, I took a short nap and then saw that I had an email from Samuel. "*Je suis bête!*" he wrote. "What was I thinking? Why didn't I just ask you to come to Brittany with me?" Then he added, in English: "Do you want?"

Of course I wanted.

Day after amazing day, Samuel did all the things that, in the movies, only the good guy does. Only the guy the girl is supposed to end up with. And he had continued to do them for three luminescent years.

So what the hell was going on now?

I woke up the morning after Samuel's fateful email about ten minutes before he was supposed to call, my stomach in one giant knot. Without getting out of bed, I opened my laptop and reread his message, hoping to discover something positive written between the lines. It did seem hopeful that Samuel hadn't been able to finish writing it. That he'd said, "I do not like it." And he did tell me that he loved me. All these signs pointed to our being able to work through this. But I hated that one poisonous sentence: "This girl is back in my life."

My phone vibrated.

"Hey," I said. I tried to let concern be the dominant note in my voice. I wanted to show Samuel that I was strong enough to handle this. Strong enough to stand by him while he worked through his feelings.

"Hi, Sharon. I got your email this morning. Thank you."

"You're welcome. I absolutely meant it. All of it. I love you very much, no matter what happens. And I'm so glad that you finally told me what was going on. I am your friend, before anything else."

"Thank you. I'm so sorry about all of this."

"I know."

I could picture him, sitting on his wrinkled blue duvet amid his Pink Floyd posters and John Lennon quotes, one hand holding the phone and the other cradling his forehead in despair.

"It's going to be okay," I told him. "It really is."

He sighed. "I hope so."

My confidence was genuine. Of course, I had no real way of knowing what was going to happen, but I found that, behind the shock and the disappointment and the worry, lurked a surprising sense of conviction: the conviction that love was going to triumph in the end.

A religious person might have called this conviction "faith." And in truth it seems very likely that, through the years, I had replaced my faith in God with faith in Love. After all, my very first worry about the God of evangelicalism had been that he didn't seem loving enough, not if he could send anyone to hell. The ironic thing was that, as I began to lose faith in the dogma of my childhood religion, I found myself relying more and more on the one character trait I believed a true God would have to possess. I developed a paradoxical sort of trust. I gave myself permission to believe what I couldn't help believing—that God wouldn't send people to hell, and that God might not even exist—and at the same time I trusted God to convince me otherwise if I was mistaken. Even in my disbelief and confusion, I prayed to know the truth. I felt that I was being as honest and sincere as I could, but even if I was deceiving myself and I was actually prideful, sinful, and rebellious, wasn't that exactly the kind of person Jesus came to save? Jesus *was* supposed to save us, wasn't he? We weren't supposed to have to save ourselves, by getting everything right on our own. And if my sin happened to be intellectual in nature, couldn't he save me from that, too? I comforted myself with the conviction that, if God existed, God would have mercy on me.

During that time—my sophomore year at Messiah College—I wrote a play about a young nihilist woman who falls in love with a dedicated Christian named John Love. Like all the writing I did in my Christian years, the play contained a conversion. The raging nihilist found God. And yet this play was different from my other stories. There was a second, contrasting conversion in it. While his wife converted to Christianity, John Love found himself overtaken by *her* former belief in the meaninglessness of life.

At night, when I would lie in bed in my college dorm room, unable to fall asleep amid the turmoil of my thoughts and feelings, I reflected back on all the efforts I'd made to please God and on all the guilt I'd felt when I'd believed there were even tiny details of my life that were unsatisfactory to him. I had always prided myself on the fact that I never feared God's being angry with me, that I knew God was compassionate and not always looking for an occasion to punish my missteps. But I realized, finally, that we can be afraid of things other than anger and punishment, and that in fact I had spent much of my life afraid of disappointing others, especially God. Sure, I believed I was forgiven for all my shortcomings because of Christ's death on the cross, but that didn't prevent me from feeling that my weaknesses still saddened my heavenly father. In fact, I'd had more than one pastor who explicitly taught that they did.

As I reflected on all my striving to please God perfectly, I realized how extremely weary I was, how disheartened and frustrated. I lay in bed and listened to the song "Give" by the Christian rock band Third Day. Over and over the lead singer pleaded with God to give him love. That's what I had always wanted to feel: God's love. I knew I couldn't earn God's approval, and I no longer had the strength even to try. But I desperately wanted God to love me anyway, for him to just forget about all of my weaknesses and possible intellectual hubris and comfort me. I whispered aloud into my tear-soaked pillow, "Please, God. Just love me."

I prayed that prayer several nights that year, but never felt any particular love in response. No warm, fuzzy feeling enveloped me. All I got was a feeling of emptiness. A feeling that no one was there.

By the time I left to study in France the following year, my doubts about Christianity had deepened. But I also couldn't see myself embracing the alternative. Belief was all I knew, and the prospect of life without God seemed terrifyingly bleak. How could life have any meaning without some sort of divine plan?

About a month after I arrived in France, my host mother took me to visit a friend of hers. She explained the visit by saying, "She's a Protestant like you." As soon as we entered her house, the friend took me into her study and started pulling books off her shelves to loan me. Knowing I was a philosophy student, she handed me works by some of France's most popular philosophers: Luc Ferry and Bernard Grasset's *L'homme-Dieu ou le Sens de la vie*, André Comte-Sponville's *Petit traité des grandes vertus*, and Pascal Bruckner's *L'euphorie perpétuelle : essai sur le devoir de bonheur*.

Back in my room at my host parents' apartment, I had only two books to keep me company. One was Victor Hugo's *Notre-Dame de Paris*, which I had lost interest in after the first five hundred pages, and the other was a philosophy anthology full of excerpts from Locke, Helvétius, and Rousseau. Even though I had no idea what to expect from the volumes this stranger was thrusting at me, I felt a keen sense of anticipation as I mentally translated the titles: *The man-God or the Meaning of life, Small treatise on the great virtues*, and *Perpetual euphoria: an essay on the duty of happiness*. When I got home, I immediately curled up on my bed and began to read.

Interestingly, all three authors were atheists. And the thing they talked about most was *l'amour*. "Only love believes in immortality," one of them wrote, quoting Eugen Drewermann. "That, we cannot learn except at the side of a person who loves us as we love them. We can only ascend to heaven by twos." I was surprised to find these atheist philosophers talking about life in such religious terms. Faced with the starkness of the material world, they were making something beautiful out of it. They were taking their humanity in all its absurdities, frailties, and bewildering joys and weaving meaning from it. Just like that. Meaning from raw human experience.

One afternoon, I was sitting in my room in my host parents' apartment, having just finished rewriting the day's class notes with the aid of a dictionary and encyclopedia, searching for words that matched the phonetics I would hastily scribble down every time the professor said something I couldn't decipher. I was in a little over my head at the Université de Nancy, but it was nice having an activity to fill the long afternoons between the end of classes and dinner with my host family at 7:30. When the strangeness of the outside world became overwhelming, I retreated to my long, narrow bedroom that resembled Van Gogh's *Bedroom in Arles*. It had the dark wood floors and the blue, yellow, and green on the walls and upholstery. The bed sat on the right side, just as in the painting, and it boasted the same massive headboard and footboard. In the evenings, the sun would set right outside the window—at about 4:30 in the afternoon, since Nancy was at the same latitude as Nova Scotia.

That particular afternoon, I finished rewriting my notes just as the sun dipped behind the apartment buildings across the way. I sat back in my wooden folding chair. I had no other pressing assignments, and I'd finished all of the books the Protestant lady had given me. The evening was as yet a blank slate. Darkness was encroaching, but instead of turning on the lamp, I retrieved a small, round metal container I'd noticed sitting on top of the bookshelf by the window. It was not much bigger than a matchbook. Popping off the lid, I found a wick set in cream-colored wax. There was a lighter in the top drawer of my desk, a freebie I'd gotten a couple of weeks ago on my first-ever trip to a bar.

I set the candle on top of the encyclopedia and, after a few false starts with the lighter, got it lit. As the flame darted upwards, it transformed my Van Gogh into a painting by Georges de la Tour: a halo of meager golden light valiantly resisting the encroaching darkness. The only thing lacking was Mary Magdalene contemplating a skull.

Under those conditions, it was hard not to find myself face to face with my innermost thoughts. Back at Messiah College, I had usually been hurrying from one activity to the next: Bible class to Music Theory to chapel to Life Fitness to ensemble rehearsal. When I had doubts about the necessity of Jesus' death on the cross or the divine inspiration of Scripture, usually all I had to do was wait a little, and the gravity of my Christian environment would pull me back into orbit. But in France I had hours upon hours in which to sit and think.

I settled myself back into my desk chair. Neatly arranged in front of me was the row of books by French philosophers, with my French Bible at the end. I reached into the top drawer of the desk and pulled out a stack of blank notebook paper. I decided I was going to write everything down. Every question that had been gnawing at me. Every Christian doctrine that offended my senses of justice and compassion. Every teaching that looked like a naked contradiction. I was going to put them all down, look them squarely in the eye, and see what I truly believed.

I knew that my parents would be devastated if I officially abandoned Christianity. I knew also that it would drastically change my relationships with my friends at Messiah College. Already Alicia and Cheryl had gotten very quiet the previous spring when I'd begun wondering aloud whether an all-good God could really send people to hell. And if I was no longer able to pray with them—prayer was our response to every crisis, whether about faith, school, or boys (usually boys)—then I didn't really see how our friendship could continue in any more than a superficial way. The pauses in our conversations would get longer and longer. The awkward stares at the ground would become more frequent. Eventually they'd stop coming around.

There was one person I thought might understand. His picture was taped to the wall above my desk. On another lonely afternoon, I'd sketched his face on a piece of notebook paper: square jaw, generous eyes behind delicately framed glasses, slightly upturned nose. Daniel had never been scared of asking difficult questions. In fact, he might have been the one to start me down that road my freshman year, asking me why I believed in six-day creationism and male headship. Since then, he'd heard me express a lot of my doubts about more fundamental doctrines, and he'd never been anything but supportive. Which made it all the more difficult to come to the realization that I stood to lose him, too. However understanding he might be, if I declared that I was actually an atheist and no longer trying to work out my differences with the Christian faith, he wouldn't be able to marry me anymore. Good Christians didn't yoke themselves to unbelievers. And, for all his understanding, Daniel was a good Christian.

Which meant that, if I left Christianity, I was leaving everyone I knew behind. And for what? I didn't know. I had no idea what lay outside Christianity. Who would I be friends with? What would we do for fun? Drugs?

I gazed into the steady flame of the candle. It made me think of Christmas, only two months away. I didn't want to give up Christmas. I didn't want to give up the walk back from the Christmas Eve service—a gaggle of cousins carrying candles over the field behind my grandparents' house. I wanted the mystery. The awe. I wanted the divine baby in the manger. The ray of hope shining from a dark, smelly stable. But I certainly didn't want hell. I didn't want a God who tortured anyone for eternity.

So that's what I wrote about, in careful cursive script: the incomprehensibility of a God who would afflict anyone—even the worst murderer—with unending agony. Jesus' death on the cross was supposed to pay the infinite debt we all owed for our willful rebellion against God, but I couldn't find any trace of this willful rebellion in me or in anyone I knew. If we did things that hurt ourselves or others, it seemed to be out of weakness or ignorance. It seemed obvious to me that who we were was a result of a great many factors that were entirely out of our control: our genes, our upbringing, the things we heard from others, the way we were rewarded with love or punished with disregard, the books we read, the thoughts that presented themselves to us as compelling and the thoughts that presented themselves as fantastical or ridiculous. All of these made us who we were. Even if we managed to "overcome" some of these influences—if we consciously chose to go against our upbringing, say—we could do it only because of *other* influences in our lives, ones that pulled us in the opposite direction. We needed something to plant the idea in us and give us the desire to pursue it. It seemed increasingly clear to me that each of us did the only thing we *could* do at that particular moment, given our exact set of circumstances, our exact knowledge, and our exact personality.

I wrote about how, given this way of looking at the world, the doctrines of sin and hell ceased to make any sense. Not only did hell look like the complete opposite of what the good God I wanted to believe in would desire, but I couldn't see how an all-good, all-powerful God would ever let creatures suffer the way they did even in this earthly life. The classic free-will defense—which said that God allowed evil in the world because it was the choice of his creatures to create it and their ability to choose freely was more important than anything else—was clearly out. And no other defense seemed available. If an all-good God existed, he obviously wasn't powerful enough to create a perfect world. And if a God existed who was powerful enough to make the world exactly as he chose, obviously he wasn't all good. But if there was no all-good, all-powerful God and there was no sin or hell for Jesus' death to redeem us from, it seemed there really was not much left of Christianity at all—not of the Christianity I'd grown up with, anyway.

Nevertheless, I closed my confession with the statement that I still *wanted* to believe. I still wanted the mystery and the awe. I still wanted Christmas and the divine baby in the manger. But not hell. Not damnation. "I want the comfort, yes, the happiness, yes, the morals, yes, the love, especially. But it seems to me that all of that is more available in the world of human beings than in prayer directed to the heavens. This is our task: to love one another. And maybe God will be content with that."

Over the previous year, I had had recurring moments in which I was overcome by intense feelings of joy. Once it was a beautiful spring day at college, when the pear trees were in full bloom and all the world felt healthy and vibrant and the possibilities endless. Another time it was a tender moment shared with Daniel. In those moments, I longed to believe in God. "Perhaps our idea of God grows out of our need to personify and tame (that is, render sympathetic) the mysteries of our universe," I now wrote. "Perhaps."

But one of the things that ended up keeping me from returning to faith—in addition to my intellectual difficulties with Christianity—was the anguish of constantly searching for an elusive "will of God." I had spent my teen years on a perpetual quest for signs directing me to what God wanted me to do with my life, long-term and on a moment-to-moment basis. Now I couldn't help feeling attracted by the possibility of freedom. Freedom to "live my life, to explore, to wonder at the mysteries, to love, and to come to a knowledge of God as *he* reveals himself, but without me tearing myself to shreds." *Is it possible?* I wondered. I was tired of trying so hard and feeling I was receiving so little in return.

At the end of two hours that afternoon in France, I had three sheets of notebook paper covered front and back with my objections to Christianity. The candle was burning low, and the wick was about to disappear beneath the surface of the pool of wax. I realized there was only one way to conclude my reflections. On the last line of the last page, I wrote a terrifying statement: "I guess I'm an atheist." And with a puff of breath, I blew out the candle.

I went to have dinner with my host parents. Lentils cooked with bacon, and toast topped with goat cheese. We watched the news and discussed the latest strikes in Paris. The *sapeurs-pompiers* wanted higher pay. What else was new?

I went back to my room and slipped into my pajamas, brushed my teeth in the little sink installed in a closet off my bedroom. Finally, I crawled into bed, pulled the duvet up to my chin, and stared into the darkness. "God?" I whispered. "I don't want to stop believing in you. You're my life. You're everything I have. Everything I *want* to have. So if you're there, will you please—just this once—give me a sign?"

It was an old refrain. I had prayed this prayer more times in the past year than I could count. But I hoped now that I simply hadn't been fervent enough. Or desperate enough. Tears began pooling in the corners of my eyes and slipping down the sides of my face to the pillow. "God, *please.* If you're there, please let me know."

I lay as still as possible, listening for a far-off roll of thunder, a rattle of the window frame, or the tiniest whisper. Even a mere feeling of warmth in my chest would have sufficed. I waited for ten minutes. But nothing out of the ordinary happened. *How could a loving God stay silent in the face of that plea?* I wondered. It seemed I had no choice but to believe that no one had heard it. So I wiped the corners of my eyes, rolled over, and went to sleep.

The next day, I wrote in my journal, "If there is a beyond, it is unknowable (for me, at present). I am too small, too limited. I wish for it, I dream of it, I hope for it, but I do not know how to believe in it. If there is a God, he's exactly the help I need." And yet no answers came.

So I guess I eventually took all of the faith and devotion I had once invested in God and invested it in earthly, human love. Salvation was not going to come from some invisible, silent God in the sky, so it was going to have to come from the love within our own breasts. Daniel had once told me, "Only God can love you the way you want to be loved." I'd found that a depressing statement coming from my fiancé. But several years later I'd discovered an almost unbelievable amount of love in my relationship with Samuel. Every day, I could feel more strongly the wondrous depth of his affection, and I felt myself giving him a love that was more unconditional than anything I'd ever known. When Samuel and I had been together only a week, we were lying in bed one night when I told him, "I could die right here and now and be content." I felt like I had finally found what I'd been searching for all those years.

And so now, when that bond was suddenly threatened, it actually seemed impossible to believe that it might break. How could something so essential to your happiness—something you might even say had "saved" you—collapse?

It couldn't.

Right?

Chapter SIX

In the days after Samuel's revelation, I spent a lot of time looking at a photograph of him that I kept by my bed. It was a picture I had taken one day when we were walking along the rocky beach near the house that Samuel's family kept on the southern coast of Brittany. It had been a chilly day, like most days in Brittany. Samuel had on his black jean jacket with the collar turned up against the wind. In the picture, he was looking off into the distance, his eyes squinting slightly. But I don't think he was looking at anything in the seascape. I think he was looking somewhere in his mind—at memories, or dreams.

Every time I looked at that picture, no matter my previous state of mind, I couldn't help feeling a deep tenderness. It reminded me of a night Samuel and I had been sitting down to dinner in our apartment in Massachusetts. Since I was still vegan then, we were probably eating some sort of bean dish. Maybe Georgian kidney beans in walnut coriander sauce. Samuel said a short blessing for the food, and then, as we began to eat, I noticed tears in his eyes.

"What's wrong?" I asked, putting my hand on top of his.

"Nothing," he said. But he pushed back his chair and went to the bookshelf where there was a box of tissues. He wiped his eyes as he settled back into his seat. "I guess I'm just starting to realize how much I love you."

So there it was. Out of the blue. Provoked by nothing more than a bowl of kidney beans in coriander. He was crying because he loved me.

And, despite everything that had happened between then and now, I still had the burning desire to comfort this man—this man who felt so much, worried so much, and kept so much inside. I knew that if he was hurting me right now, it was only because he himself was hurting. That's when we cause pain to those we love: when we ourselves are in distress. I wanted to soothe that pain. Wanted him to know that the deep connection we had built over the years was not in vain, that it would sustain us in a difficult time like this. That it would allow us to emerge joyful and triumphant on the other side.

I did wonder, of course, exactly what kinds of worries were on Samuel's mind. The day after his revelatory email, he told me in our phone conversation that he felt as though seeing this girl again—and feeling the feelings he had for her—was just one more sign that our wedding was not meant to be.

"One *more*?" I asked. "What were the others?"

"Filiberto," he replied.

Filiberto was a friend of Samuel's, a Mexican priest. Samuel had met him years ago as a teenager, on a trip to the Sinai Desert in Egypt. They'd remained in contact ever since. The first year Samuel and I were together, Filiberto came to France and visited us at the farm in

Brittany. He was a calm, quiet fellow. Wiser than his forty years. Samuel saw him as a spiritual guide as well as a friend. When Filiberto left to go home, he told Samuel, "Take good care of Sharon."

Samuel had taken Filiberto's words as a blessing on our relationship. And when we got engaged, he told me he wanted Filiberto to do the wedding. Actually, he put it this way: "If Filiberto doesn't do the wedding, I can't get married."

So, as soon as we returned from our engagement trip to the British Isles, Samuel started trying to get ahold of Filiberto in Mexico. We didn't want to set the date until we were sure he could make it. But when Samuel called the community where Filiberto lived and spoke to them in his rudimentary Spanish, he discovered that Filiberto was away in Canada and wouldn't be back for at least a week. They weren't sure when. Samuel left a message and waited and waited for Filiberto to call back, but no call came.

Finally, Samuel called again. Yes, Filiberto was back from Canada, but he was very busy. "When is a good time to call?" Samuel asked. He was given a time, but still, every time he dialed, Filiberto was out. And he never called back.

"He's just busy," I told Samuel. "And it's probably complicated to figure out how to call France from Mexico."

"No, it's not. He's done it before."

I knew Filiberto, and I knew he wouldn't purposely be avoiding talking to Samuel, but Samuel started wondering if their failure to get in touch was a sign that the wedding might not be a good idea after all.

"You're being superstitious," I told him. "Whether you and your friend have trouble getting ahold of each other has nothing to do with whether or not we should get married."

"He's not just a friend. Filiberto is the one who brought me back to God, and I need his blessing on our wedding. He knows how important this is to me."

I just shook my head and hoped Filiberto wouldn't wait too long.

Finally, a week before I had to fly back to the States, we got a call from Mexico. "I'm very busy around *Navidad*," Filiberto told Samuel. We'd been planning to have our wedding between Christmas and New Year's, because it was the most convenient time for my family to travel. "I have to go to several different towns to do Mass. But I will see what I can do to fit in a trip to France."

Two weeks later—after Samuel had seen his high-school friend and said he couldn't marry me, but before he'd told me why—he got another call from Filiberto. Filiberto told him he couldn't swing the December wedding. "Why don't you go ahead and get married in December?" Filiberto suggested. "And then in January or February I'll come to France and give you a blessing?"

I thought it sounded like a great compromise. But now Samuel told me it wasn't good enough. It was another sign that things were wrong.

"Samuel," I told him. "This is *your* decision. This is about what *you* want to do, not about what you think the universe is telling you to do."

"We can't always have what we want," he replied. "That's not what life is about."

Clearly, Samuel was very confused. And with anyone else, I would probably have seethed with frustration. With Daniel, for example, I might have made some very cutting remarks about irrationality. But Samuel was different. I had my own dedicated well of patience for him, and it went very, very deep.

So I decided that the best thing I could do was simply to find a way to pass the time until Samuel sorted everything out. Of course, this was easier said than done. From the moment Samuel and I hung up the phone the morning after his big email, the temporal dimension began to stretch itself out like an elastic band. Seconds felt like minutes. Minutes like hours. And hours like entire weeks.

I wasn't the sort of person who normally had trouble finding things to do. When I was ten years old, I had pleaded with my mother to homeschool me so I would have time for all the things I wanted to accomplish: writing novels, drafting house plans, growing vegetables, writing computer programs, learning Mandarin Chinese—the things I considered my "real" work. As an adult, I was no different. One of the reasons I'd left academia was that I couldn't stand spending forty hours a week doing what *other* people considered important. I still had too many unmet goals of my own: to write yet another novel, to learn everything I could about farming, to can an entire winter's worth of vegetables, to learn to speak Breton, to make a solar cooker, to raise chickens. I had so much energy, so much ambition, and what I wanted, most of the time, was just to be left alone. This was one of the things Samuel and I had initially bonded over. He had been perpetually amazed when I suggested we spend an evening reading. "*T'es sûre?*" he'd ask. "You're not just saying that to make me happy?"

Samuel and I had spent countless evenings happily reading alongside each other. But now, no book could hold my attention. All of my mental energy was consumed with thinking about when Samuel would realize his true feelings and things would go back to normal. I carried my phone with me everywhere in my parents' house, constantly hoping that, in the next minute, Samuel would call and say he was ready to marry me again.

Eventually, I found an occupation for myself. A physical task as repetitive as my thoughts. Four years ago, my mom and sisters and I had started making a wedding quilt for my sister Rebecca and her then-fiancé Ryan. Even though they'd now celebrated their three-year anniversary, the quilt was still stretched out on a quilting frame in the spare bedroom upstairs, awaiting the completion of the last and most time-consuming step in the process. After wandering around the house for days unable to occupy myself, I sat down and began stitching together the layers of cloth and batting. In and out. In and out. In diagonal lines across three hundred twelve multicolored triangles. With my cell phone on the dresser nearby.

That's where I was when Samuel called me in the middle of the day Tuesday. Two days after the fateful email. "How are you?" I asked cautiously.

"I'm feeling more confident," he said.

"About what?" I thought I knew what he meant—that he was more confident about marrying me—but I had learned that, in a cross-cultural relationship, it was very important to get everything spelled out. When Samuel and I had first started dating, I'd more than once been stopped dead in my tracks when he'd said to me, in English, "I have something to tell you." My heart would start thumping wildly, expecting the disclosure of some momentous secret. But then Samuel would come out with some innocuous historical anecdote. "Legend says Merlin was born in Brittany's Forêt de Brocéliande," he would say. Or, "Benjamin Franklin landed in Brittany when he came to ask the French for money for the War of Independence." Finally, I'd had to tell him that, when Americans wanted to introduce these kinds of facts, we said, "Want to hear something interesting?"

Now, before jumping to any conclusions, positive or negative, I wanted explicit confirmation. "You're feeling more confident about *what*?" I repeated.

"About the wedding," he said.

Well then.

When we hung up a few minutes later, I ate my first real meal in four days. And I could actually taste it. The bread. The mustard. The turkey lunch meat. The oil and salt on the Ruffles potato chips. Afterward, I went back to working on the quilt, but with new resolve.

I was going to finish Ryan and Rebecca's quilt as quickly as possible so I could start on one for me and Samuel. I could already see it: pure white with luxurious amounts of stitching in the shapes of rings and chains and Celtic knots. We would keep it on a four-poster bed in the apartment I'd been designing for us.

After we'd announced that we were getting married, Samuel's dad told us he would give us an entire wing of the farmhouse to remodel into an apartment. We could live there until we had children. Then Samuel's dad would give us the main part of the house, and he'd take the apartment.

The day after he told us this, I pulled out the tape measure and went to work. We had about a thousand square feet, spread over two floors. Downstairs, in place of the current study and guest bedroom, we'd put a combination living/dining room space. Next to that, in what used to be the farm's walk-in refrigerator, we'd put the kitchen. And off that would be a laundry room and bathroom. Above, we'd have a large master bedroom with a cathedral ceiling and the old, hand-hewn beams of the stable left exposed above our heads. I could see Samuel and me waking up early to the sound of the rooster and sliding out from under the warm wedding quilt to throw on our clothes and pad down the steps to the kitchen. Samuel would put the coffee on. I'd stir up some muffins and stick them in the oven before heading outside to feed and water the chickens. Then we'd work together all day, each of us at our own desk, writing to our hearts' content. I'd only stop for a couple of hours in the afternoon to teach piano lessons—since we had to have a little money for food and electricity.

There's an expression in French: *vivre d'amour et d'eau fraîche*. Living on love and water. That's pretty much what we intended to do.

And, honestly, I didn't care if we were poor in money. Money mattered very little to me. What I craved was *time*. Time to throw myself into writing, gardening, and puzzling out the secrets of the universe. I wanted to be rich in all the things money couldn't buy. Soul-rich. And Samuel wanted the same things. Minus the gardening.

After Samuel's declaration that he was feeling more confident, I spent the rest of the day quilting and dreaming about our future together. It was so good to be back in a place where all of it again felt possible. Indeed, felt just around the corner.

The next morning, Samuel called me at 7am sounding positively cheerful. "I'm driving down to the beach!" he announced gaily. I could hear the Renault's engine chugging in the background.

His dad's beach house was where Samuel went to get away and work on his books, far from nosy family members and neighbors. The little townhouse was just a three-minute walk from the ocean, and in the off-season of mid-September, it was a great place for solitude, reflection, and coming to one's senses. It also had the advantage of being far away from Her.

"Great!" I said. "How long are you planning on staying down there?"

"A few days. We'll see." His optimistic tone was music to my ears. I didn't know what had changed, but I wasn't going to pry, for fear of jinxing it. "Listen," he said. "I'm on the road. I'll call you later."

"Okay, baby. Have a good trip!"

I got up, got dressed, and sat down to work on the quilt again with an incredible feeling of hope. Samuel and I had been tested, and our love had been found strong. In the face of the greatest threat a relationship could encounter, I had stayed calm, I had let Samuel work through his feelings, and now—*voilà*—things were returning to normal. All of this we would soon remember as just a momentary blip on the radar screen of our lives. Samuel sounded so much better—so much more like *himself* again—that I bet that, when he called me back in a few hours, he'd be ready to reset the date for the wedding.

The only thing was, he didn't call back.

Morning turned into late morning. Late morning turned into early afternoon. France was six hours ahead of Virginia, so as four o'clock approached, I knew that the likelihood that Samuel would call again that day was growing slimmer and slimmer. I had so been looking forward to talking to him and having everything resolved that I knew I couldn't wait through another entire night to hear his voice. I dug my phone card out of my wallet.

Samuel's phone rang five times and then went to voice mail. He was probably driving. Or in the shower. Or talking to his dad. "Hey, it's me," I said to the machine. "Just wondering what you were up to. Give me a call when you get this so I can tell you good night. Love you."

Samuel usually called me back within ten or fifteen minutes. Thirty at most. I tried to read a book, but I glanced at the clock so often I kept losing my place. I saw an hour pass. Then another.

I sat down to dinner with my family. My mom had made chicken and dumplings with plenty of extra dumplings, but I could barely swallow. What was going on? Samuel had never not called when he said he would.

I began to worry about him all alone in the townhouse at the beach. What if something had happened to him? What if he'd slipped and fallen getting out of the shower and was lying unconscious on the floor of the *salle de bains*? That shower curtain had always been too long. Or what if he'd never even made it to the beach? What if he'd had a car accident on the way down, just minutes after I talked to him?

When I crawled into bed that night, still without any word, my worries took a new, malicious turn. What if he was with *Her*? What if she had joined him down at the beach house, and they were at this very moment carrying on an intimate conversation late into the night? I imagined them sitting at the wooden table across from the kitchenette, their heads pressed close to one another as they shared stories from their high-school days. Maybe they were laughing. Or crying. It didn't matter. That was *my* place at that table beside Samuel. Not hers. *Not hers.*

I don't know how I managed to fall asleep with such an image in my mind, but every so often, I would open my eyes to find that yet another hour had passed and still I had received no calls. The closer the clock crept toward morning, the more convinced I was that She was the most likely explanation. And yet it didn't make any sense. Why would he be seeing her again when he had just told me he was feeling more confident about marrying me?

Eventually, I awoke to a window full of daylight. I checked my phone. No missed calls. No messages. I got out of bed and tiptoed downstairs to the computer, embarrassed that everyone in the house knew how early I got up to check my email. But there was nothing from Samuel.

By ten o'clock, when I still hadn't heard anything, I became convinced that the most probable explanation was an accident. It simply wasn't like Samuel not to get back to me, even if he *had* been with her last night. If it was a car accident, I reasoned, the police would have called his dad, the owner of the car. And his dad would have called me. But what if his dad couldn't find my number? I had given it to him over a year ago. He could have misplaced it. And what if it wasn't a car accident? If Samuel had collapsed in the beach house, no one would know for a long time. He didn't talk to his dad on the phone every day, so his dad might not know anything was wrong for a while yet. *I can't just sit here*, I thought. *I've got to call his dad.*

I dug in my wallet for the little slip of paper on which I'd written his phone number. Before I dialed, I checked my email one last time. And, this time, there was a message from Samuel. A very short one. "I'm sorry for not calling you back," he said. "I wasn't capable of talking to you. I'm still not sure I am."

At first, I was simply relieved to know he was alive. Relieved that he was communicating something—anything—to me. But, almost immediately, my relief turned to anger. Hadn't he known how torturous it would be for me to wait almost twenty-four hours for him to return my phone call? I understood that he might be uncomfortable talking to me if he had seen Her again. He probably had no idea what to say. But didn't he have enough regard for my feelings to at least send some sort of message, like, "I'm okay. I just can't talk right now"?

There was only one other time in our relationship when I had ever doubted Samuel's concern for me. The previous spring, he'd been in France for a month and a half and was supposed to be coming back to the States to finish out the school year with me. I thought he'd be back in Boston in time to see Rebecca and Ryan, who were using their spring break from seminary to come visit. But they came and went, and Samuel still didn't arrive. "He's got a lot to do with his new book coming out," I told them.

Samuel said it might take another week or so for him to be ready to fly over. But two weeks went by, and he still hadn't bought any tickets. "When are you coming?" I asked him one day on the phone.

"Do you think maybe you could come here instead?"

"How? I have to teach." I was in the middle of my spring semester.

"You could come when you have your week off at Passover," suggested Samuel. Brandeis was a Jewish-sponsored university—another example of how, even as an atheist, I always seemed to find myself surrounded by spirituality.

"That's still three weeks away!" I protested. "I told you last year I couldn't do any more separations of two months." The year before, we'd been apart for a full eight weeks, and by the fifth week, the separation had become excruciating. I'd gone to visit my friends Debbie and Alicia for a few days but broke down crying when it was time for bed and I was once again all alone. "Never again," I told him then. "I simply cannot do two months again."

But he seemed to have forgotten that episode. "I just have so much to do with my book," he was saying. "I need to do publicity. Try to get some magazine coverage. Talk to people."

"Samuel, you *said* you would come in March."

"I know. But I *can't*."

I tried to stay calm, but I was beginning to suspect he just didn't care. With as much dignity as I could muster, I told him, "Samuel, I need you."

"You'll be okay. There are things I have to do here."

"There are things I want to do, too!" I almost yelled. "I want to start my farm when I finish at Brandeis in May. But you want me to come to Brittany, even though you can't commit to making a life there yet. You're asking me to sacrifice the thing I *most* want. Can't you sacrifice *something*? Can't you find some way to work on your book from here?"

"I don't know…."

"I *need* you, Samuel. Please just come!" I started sobbing.

"I'm hanging up," he said. "I can't listen to you cry."

"Don't hang up!" I pleaded. "*S'il te plaît.*"

"I'll call you back in a little while." Click.

I can do this, I said to myself. *He has legitimate reasons to want to be in France right now. I can make the sacrifice. I can go over there at Passover.*

When he called back about ten minutes later, I was calm. "Hi."

"Hi."

Silence hung in the air for a moment. Then, in a quiet voice full of concern, he said, "If I come next Tuesday, will it be soon enough?"

"Yes," I replied. "Yes, it will."

That was the only other time I'd felt like Samuel simply wasn't taking my feelings into account. And, in the end, he had proven that he really did care. He had come like he said he would.

But now he was suddenly much more distant than that. It was as though, in the space of twenty-four hours, he had floated out into another universe where his attachment to me didn't matter at all anymore. Twenty-four hours ago, he had said he was feeling more confident about marrying me, and now he felt he had no responsibility even to return my calls.

"What's going on?" I asked him the next day, when he finally felt "able" to talk again. "Please just tell me what you're thinking, even if it's something you think is going to hurt me. I feel hurt already being so in the dark."

"I don't know, Sharon."

"You don't know what?"

"What I'm thinking."

"Well, what do you *feel?*"

"I don't know. Tired." He did sound beaten down. Defeated.

"Remember that I'm your best friend, and I only want what's best for you. Have you talked to anyone about this? Someone besides me? Or…this girl?"

"No. No one knows."

I sighed. I was sure that hiding these things from his family was responsible for a lot of the stress Samuel felt. I knew that, when I was going through a difficult time, if I just talked to someone else about it, the problem seemed a lot easier to handle.

"Talk to your dad," I said. "Or your sister." *Someone who will reassure you that these are normal doubts and you shouldn't give up on the best relationship you've ever had.*

I knew I was the best relationship Samuel had ever had because he'd told me so. "I've never felt this way before," he'd said. Just like the line from the Coldplay song we'd sung on that long-ago night after the apple harvest. "You understand me," he'd said. "You know me better than anyone."

I had long worn that phrase like a badge of honor. And now, even in the midst of this confusion, it comforted me. Whatever Samuel was experiencing, whatever momentary questions he had, I had his word that *I* was the one who knew him better than anyone. And he would come back to that, I was sure.

For a week, Samuel and I carried on strained phone conversations. I continued to urge him to talk to someone. Someone with no stake in the outcome of all this. Someone he could trust to help him see clearly. But he hemmed and hawed. He was embarrassed, I think. Embarrassed to tell his father and sister about his doubts, about his straying feelings, about everything he was putting me through. And I couldn't say very much, because *I* was embarrassed, too. I hadn't told anyone about the reason behind Samuel's doubts. Not my family. Not even my best friends. It felt too degrading.

Then, a week after the episode in which Samuel didn't return my calls, it happened again. It started with him not calling me in the morning like he usually did. I waited patiently, wanting to give him time and space if he needed it. I didn't call him that day until it was evening in France. He didn't answer the phone, so I left a message. And then I waited. And waited. And waited.

This time, at least, I didn't worry that he'd been in a car accident or knocked himself unconscious falling out of the shower. This time I knew from the beginning exactly what he was doing: talking to Her.

Of course, that didn't make me much calmer. In fact, as I lay in bed trying to sleep, I felt as though my heart was literally going to explode out of my chest. I'd always thought that "heartache" was just an expression, but this pain was not metaphorical at all. Was it possible that I could have a heart attack at the age of twenty-nine? It was probably not very likely, but all this stress couldn't be good for my health. Even if nothing happened to me now, down the road all the wear and tear of the past few weeks was bound to have an effect. I loved Samuel, and I wanted the best for him, but I decided I would be very upset if his behavior ended up sending me to an early grave.

Finally, after a full twenty-four hours of non-responsiveness, Samuel wrote to me. Maybe it would be better, he said, for us to communicate by email for a while.

It had been weeks since I'd been able to see his face, touch his skin, feel his breath on my cheek. Now I wasn't going to be able to hear his voice, either? This road was turning out to be a hell of a lot longer than I'd expected.

Chapter SEVEN

It took a day or two, but I finally realized that, as hard as it was for me to focus on anything but waiting for Samuel to recover his sanity, I really needed to. I needed to put the quilt aside for a while and find something more mentally engaging.

So I decided to take myself out for coffee. Just like I used to do in Paris.

There weren't many choices for coffee in the rural county where my parents lived. Even driving to town thirty minutes away, there was really only one place that came close to simulating the feel of a big-city coffee shop. It sat at the intersection of the two largest streets—each only two lanes wide—and had wooden benches and red metal tables lining the brick sidewalk out front. It was the end of September, and the weather was still T-shirt warm, so I carried my mug of organic

French roast out to the sidewalk and set myself up at the best table, the one from which I could see up and down three spokes of the intersection and watch all the college students and Civil War enthusiasts go by.

I pulled out the book I'd brought with me, tucked into the black Ecole Normale Supérieure satchel I still carried. Maybe it was snobby to walk around with a satchel marked, "Rue d'Ulm, Paris," but it was one concrete connection I still had to the life that was slowly slipping through my fingers, and I felt more intact when I had it by my side.

The book was a collection of essays about my favorite author, Wendell Berry. I'd had it for months and had yet to open it. Today seemed like a good day. If anything could get me out of my funk, it was probably a book about the man who had inspired me to become what I was now: a free-wheeling intellectual liberated from the institutional demands of academia.

I discovered Wendell Berry in my first year out of grad school, when I was just beginning my postdoctoral fellowship at Brandeis University outside Boston. My position at Brandeis was one I'd sort of fallen into. When I'd started dating Samuel, I'd had one year left of my doctoral program at NYU, and I'd been sorely tempted to leave behind everything I'd been working towards and make myself an entirely new life in France. In fact, I'd even been offered a job in Paris. One afternoon, I'd been strolling through the neighborhood of Montparnasse when I came across a showroom for a company that designed kitchens and bathrooms. I'd always enjoyed home design and had spent a fair amount of time as a teenager drawing house plans, so I ducked inside to see what they had on display. The manager struck up a conversation with me and, when he found out I did architectural drawing as a hobby, offered me a job on the spot. He even offered to help me get a work visa. But I was too responsible to take him up on it. For better or worse, I felt obliged to return to the States and finish my degree. After all, I had a complete draft of my dissertation, one that just needed some revising here and there. Why not stick things out just a little longer and emerge with the title of "Doctor"?

But then, once I was back in the States, it also seemed natural to go ahead and apply for academic jobs for the following year. Everyone else in my program was doing it. As long as I was going to the trouble of finishing my degree, why not see what it could get me? So I sent in sixty-five applications for university positions. A pretty standard number, believe it or not. From those sixty-five applications, I gleaned ten interviews, three fly-outs to visit campuses, and two job offers. The offer I accepted, at Brandeis, was actually my third choice of all sixty-five positions I applied for. It was a two-year postdoctoral fellowship in ethics, my area of specialization, and it required teaching only a single course per semester.

The day after I defended my dissertation in New York, Samuel and I headed north to find ourselves an apartment in Waltham, Massachusetts, a suburb just a fifteen-minute train ride from Boston. It was a delightful town, and we found an apartment within walking distance of Brandeis, as well as within walking distance of all the stores, restaurants, and coffee shops we could need. Commuting to my office on foot actually took less time there than when I'd been living in Manhattan. And when the weather was fine, Samuel and I could take a stroll on the Charles River Walk or hike up Prospect Hill, from which we could see Boston's skyscrapers. Often we rode the train or the bus into the city and spent time strolling the campuses of Harvard and MIT, or circling Boston Common and exploring the historic streets of the North End and Beacon Hill.

But we didn't have any problem staying home, either. Our apartment in Waltham was on the second and third floors of an old house, nestled in the leaves and branches of a stand of sugar maples. The trees cast enough shade that, even without an air conditioner, the place was never uncomfortably hot in summer, even when outdoor temperatures would get into the nineties. We'd leave the windows open several months a year, and I loved feeling the breeze and hearing the sounds of children and birds and the pitter-patter of rain on a gray day. Samuel and I would sit for meals at an old wooden dining table I'd found at an antique store, and we'd eat food freshly prepared from the farmers' market while we listened to the leaves rustling outside the window, the crickets singing, or our Guatemalan neighbors enjoying a cookout. Even indoors, we were wonderfully connected to the outside world. And the house itself seemed to have a presence. Full of light and love.

It seemed like a very fitting place to live while I taught my courses at Brandeis, one of which was on the subject of utopian communities. I'd designed the course myself, as a combination philosophy/sociology course that focused on groups like the Shakers, Oneida, and the Hutterites—people throughout American history who had attempted to create working examples of their ideal human society. In Waltham, I actually felt like I was living in a place as close to utopia as I'd ever gotten.

And my job at Brandeis was a great one, by the standards of academia. It offered a solid salary and a great deal of flexibility in my research. I don't think I could have imagined anything better, really. The discontent I felt growing in me was not a result of my particular situation. It was an effect of academia as a whole. And of my insatiable idealism.

I had been hired by Brandeis to teach ethics. My course on utopian communities came under that umbrella, as did my courses on utilitarianism and on truth and objectivity in ethics. But the problem was that I didn't believe ethics was something you could learn in a classroom. At the time, the most famous philosophical essay on the morality of abortion compared an unwanted pregnancy to being involuntarily hooked up by an IV to a world-class violinist who would die without this bizarre form of life support. Such fantastic thought experiments were the bread and butter of philosophical ethics, but I couldn't see how discussing such unrealistic situations would help students when they or their girlfriends accidentally got pregnant. Nor could I see what bearing it should have on public policy decisions. The abstract, highly theoretical discussions of the philosophy classroom left out so much of what mattered in the real world.

The more I thought about the aims of my courses, the more I began to think that ethics was something you could only learn by living, and by living in the orbit of other people who dealt admirably with the complex choices of daily life. Teaching ethics in a classroom, with a textbook and essay exams, seemed like a scam. A scam my students were paying almost thirty thousand dollars a year for. "Take your thirty thousand dollars," I wanted to tell them, "and go find someone whose life you thoroughly admire. Pay them thirty thousand dollars to let you work alongside them for a year. You'll learn way more of value than you'd ever learn sitting here listening to me."

Thinking those kinds of thoughts, while sitting in the ivory tower of academia, made me feel very lonely. Questioning the legitimacy of the institution that was the livelihood of all my colleagues and in which my students' families had already invested tens of thousands of dollars wasn't something I could do out loud, not without feeling ungrateful and self-righteous.

It was while I was first wrestling with these doubts and feeling my isolation from the professional academic world that I read my first essay by Wendell Berry. My brother-in-law had mentioned his name to me. "I think you'd like him because he writes a lot about the environment and local economies," he said. Then he added, somewhat apologetically, "He is a Luddite, though."

I'd learned the meaning of the term 'Luddite' just weeks before, while reading *Better Off*, a book written by a guy named Eric Brende who went to live for a year and a half in an Amish-like community. A Luddite was someone who was skeptical of the value of modern technology, and little did my brother-in-law know, but that was right up my alley.

Samuel and I lived a bit like Luddites ourselves. We had purposely decided not to own a car in Waltham. And when our apartment didn't come with a washing machine, I bought a fifty-dollar hand-cranked version, which Samuel and I took turns using, dripping our clothes dry on a rack over the old iron bathtub. We washed our clothes by hand, our dishes by hand, and only rarely broke the television out of storage, when there was a specific video we wanted to watch. We didn't even have an internet connection.

As you might imagine, I bought the first Wendell Berry volume I could get my hands on. And by the second page of *Sex, Economy, Freedom and Community*, I knew I was in the presence of a kindred spirit. "[T]he new commercial education is fun for everybody," wrote Berry sarcastically. "All you have to do in order to have or to provide such an education is to pay your money (in advance) and master a few simple truths." These included: "Educated people are more valuable than other people because education is a value-adding industry," "The sign of exceptionally smart people is that they speak a language that is intelligible only to other people in their 'field' or only to themselves," and "Computers make people even better and smarter than they were made by previous thingamabobs. Or if some people prove incorrigibly wicked or stupid or both, computers will at least speed them up."

Berry was a farmer as well as a writer, and, as someone else who found plants and animals to be indispensable companions, I bet that it was partly his acquaintance with the complexities of the practical, physical world that helped him to articulate so brilliantly my own nascent thoughts on the hollowness of a university education. What was sure was that I no longer felt alone. In the space of two pages, I had found a soul mate.

The problem, of course, was what to do about my life.

I was trying my best to be true to my ideals within the confines of the university. My students at Brandeis were enthusiastic, hardworking, and often even more idealistic than I was. I wanted so much to respect their earnestness by teaching them in the most authentic way I knew how. I ached to take them out to a farm or into the woods and say, "This is *real* life. Let's work on understanding what's going on *here*." When I could, I did hold our lectures outside. We discussed Thoreau's *Walden* while sitting in a circle on a grassy hill on the south side of campus. And I demonstrated for my students my hand-cranked washing machine, as well as the solar cooker I'd built from cardboard and aluminum foil for a total of fifteen cents. They were fascinated. How could something so useful be so simple? And so cheap?

But I wanted to do so much more. I wanted to talk about the ethics of meat eating while we slaughtered chickens. I wanted to talk about the insanity of corporate America while we spun yarn, tanned leather, or built a house. Yet the insurance requirements of the university made the cost of the most minor field trips prohibitive. The classroom started to feel like a jail.

I thought about these matters on my walk to and from work every day. I loved the fact that my commute—fifteen minutes, door to door—involved observing the slow evolution of the trees, shrubs, and flowers along my path. I gave myself time to stop and sniff lilac blossoms. To stoop down and try to identify a beautiful plant I'd never noticed in Virginia, which turned out to be a New England aster. Or to marvel at some edible-looking berries growing on a tree. Mulberries, perhaps?

One morning I tried to find an even more scenic route to my office. Instead of walking down South Street, I took off through a park and into some woods that backed up to the northern boundary of the university. I scrambled up a hill and found the campus without trouble. But I was disappointed to discover that there was a chain-link fence solidly guarding the perimeter. *Is this to keep people out or in?* I wondered. *Do I want to teach at an institution that so visibly marks its division from the world around it?*

Each day I arrived in my office more depressed, knowing that it was not where I wanted to be but not sure if I could leave. Since I'd started questioning my desire for a career in philosophy, I'd been plagued by self-doubt. What if the real reason I wanted out of philosophy was that it was too hard? Or that I was too lazy to do the necessary work? I worried that my desire to leave academia was just an example of the grass's always being greener on the other side. Was I naïve to think I could find something better than this already very privileged work situation? Didn't every career demand compromise and frustration, at least some of the time?

I thought back to the beginning of my interest in philosophy. I hadn't started out a philosophy major in college. I hadn't even known what philosophy was when I arrived at Messiah. I declared my major as music, because I'd taken piano lessons for years, composed my own pieces now and then, and figured music was as good as either of the other majors I was considering: theater and French. Even though I loved to write—and had been writing novels and screenplays since middle school—I never considered a major in English. My mother had majored in English, and I couldn't see myself obsessing over grammar the way she did, or dissecting Shakespeare as she'd made me do when she homeschooled me.

So I started out studying music. And then, my sophomore year, because it was required for graduation, I took a philosophy course. I quickly discovered that philosophy was an area of study devoted to the deep questions I had always pondered in my spare time, questions like, "What's the ultimate nature of the universe?" or "What makes certain things right and others wrong?" or even, "What's the *meaning* of the phrase 'the meaning of life'?" I did very well in that class. So well that the professor approached me about becoming a philosophy major. And it was good timing, because I was already starting to feel bored with music. By my second year in the program, I could only make myself practice piano for ten minutes at a time, with five-minute breaks for reading philosophy or scribbling down dialogue for a play.

I knew that the purpose of majoring in philosophy would be to go to graduate school. And that the purpose of going to graduate school would be to become a professor. It was the first time I'd ever considered a career in academia, but it seemed to fit. After all, it would be a way for me to write about the nature of the universe *and* have a reliable income. Recently, I'd been considering supporting my writing career by waiting tables at Pizza Hut. I had worked there over the summer and hadn't found it half bad. But when my professor told me that PhD programs in philosophy actually paid students to attend, I was sold.

Nevertheless, it wasn't just the money that enticed me. I really did adore doing philosophy as an undergrad. Especially in my senior year, when I put together a string of independent studies. During the three weeks of January Term senior year, I had no classes at all and probably read twenty books. I'd wake up early, sometimes even before the sun was up, and settle myself at the dining table of our campus apartment, reading and taking notes all day long, usually until I noticed the sun had already gone down again and I'd forgotten to eat lunch. When I did remember to eat, it was something quick. Like a microwaved bean burrito. Or lima beans straight from the can. I perpetually wished for more time and energy. And my roommate Alicia said she never saw me happier than when I was returning from the library with a new round of reading material stacked to my chin.

When acceptances to grad schools started rolling in, I took them as another sign that I was on the right track. And after making a few campus visits, I settled on New York University—home to one of my favorite philosophers, Thomas Nagel. He'd published an article on the meaning of life, and I thought that boded well for my ability to do the kind of philosophy that interested me. It didn't hurt, either, that NYU's philosophy department was ranked number one worldwide in analytic philosophy. But the clincher was that NYU's philosophy PhD program had the fewest requirements of any I'd looked at. Minimal class requirements. No comprehensive exams. Exactly the freedom I was looking for.

The reality, of course, was somewhat different than I expected. The NYU philosophy program did offer a lot of liberty, which I took full advantage of, but at the same time there was a marked difference in atmosphere from Messiah College. I found that, when you discussed philosophy with the students and professors there, everything you said had to be couched in terms of some established philosophical theory or they were unable—or maybe just unwilling—to understand. I realized after a few months that this graduate school was designed to produce a very particular sort of philosopher, and that I wasn't sure it was the kind I wanted to be, even if that's what it took to be at the "top" of my field.

But, again, it was hard for me to know whether the antipathy I was starting to feel towards professional philosophy was due to its own deficiencies or mine. Was the reason that I suddenly found myself with nothing to say during department colloquia really that I thought about things so differently from everyone else? Or was I just not smart enough to formulate my thoughts quickly and clearly? For the first time, I was a small fish in a big pond. Might that be the real reason for my diminishing interest in philosophy? That it wasn't so easy anymore?

I wished I could have played the game of professional philosophy to perfection and *then* rejected it. That would have been more reassuring. But becoming a world-class philosopher wasn't just going to happen. It was going to require a lot of effort. If only I could know for sure how much of my reticence to put in that effort was due to valid reservations about the profession and how much was due to fear. Or plain old-fashioned laziness.

When I got to Brandeis, I did my best to pursue the philosophical ideas that still interested me, to see whether I could carve out a place for myself in the profession. The job at Brandeis was a real opportunity, I realized. It gave me the best experience of academia I could imagine: a small but well-reputed university with great students and faculty, the chance to teach exactly the courses I wanted, and a majority of my time free for my own research. In fact, the conditions were so good that I knew that, if I wasn't satisfied there, I wouldn't be satisfied anywhere in the ivory tower.

So I taught my courses on ethics and utopian communities, and I wrote and presented a couple of what felt to me like daring papers. One of them was on the possibility that human intelligence doesn't make us superior to other living things. I was intensely interested in the topic but found it difficult to explore while meeting the expectations for professional philosophy papers. It felt like translating this idea into philosophical jargon sucked the life out of it. Also, analytic philosophers expected *arguments*: some way of leading readers step by step down a logical path from their current beliefs to the ones the writer wants to convince them of. But I wasn't interested in finding a way to reason from people's current beliefs to the one I was suggesting. I suspected that the values and beliefs that underlay much of contemporary Western society were faulty, and I wanted to explore an alternative paradigm, showing its internal coherence and perhaps prompting readers to reflect on whether they had solid reasons for maintaining their current view over this very different one that was every bit as rational, and much less demeaning to the rest of life on earth. Unfortunately, the more my views began to diverge from the mainstream, the more insistently I felt the need to free my intellectual and creative pursuits from the expectations of a conservative, respectable institution like the university.

But was it just a cop-out? I mean, if I wanted to change the world, wasn't the university the place to do it? The place where the minds of the next generation were being formed? Was I just fooling myself in thinking I could find happiness and meaningful work outside academia?

While growing increasingly dizzy on this merry-go-round of questions, I read another of Wendell Berry's works, an essay titled "A Native Hill." Until I read that essay, I had assumed that Berry had always known he was supposed to be a farmer as well as a writer. That God had whispered his calling to him as a child and he had never thought of doing anything else. But, in the first few pages of "A Native Hill," I learned that he'd actually started out as an academic, with a very promising career in English literature. He said it was only after "considerable difficulty and doubt and hard thought" that he decided to leave the academic fast-track and take a teaching job in his home state of Kentucky, a job that would allow him to move back to his hometown and farm. It seemed significant to me that the school where he'd happened to be teaching when he made this decision was NYU.

When Berry left New York, his colleagues warned him that his decision would squander his literary gifts and relegate him to obscurity. But, despite Berry's reluctance to promote himself, over the years his novels, essays, and poems gained him an impressive literary and cultural following. Many years later, he was not only a well-respected writer but an adored spokesperson for the newest generation of back-to-the-landers. He was a living, breathing example of someone who had forsaken the ivory tower for a more meaningful life of writing and manual labor and had actually found it.

And still I hesitated. Wendell Berry was an exceptional man, after all. A writer of great wisdom and inimitable literary style. What did his success have to do with my own prospects? *He* might have been able to make himself a career without being affiliated with a prestigious university, but could I?

In my second fall at Brandeis, the end of my fellowship was in sight, and it was time for me to apply for a new position elsewhere. The stress of my decision intensified, and, unfortunately, the stress didn't make my thinking on the issue any clearer. Finally, I remembered an old decision-making technique of mine. The whole of the technique was this: to purposely abstain from thinking about the matter at hand. The idea was to relax the mind so that the right answer could bubble up from the unconscious in its own good time.

Thus, for two days, I resolutely refrained from thinking about my future. On the third day, I was sitting in my office at Brandeis finishing up a paper to submit for publication in a journal when I suddenly realized, with startling clarity, that I simply could not spend the rest of my life glued to a desk chair and writing papers that were of no interest to 99.9 percent of the world, including me. Such a path promised me no joy. And there were too many other things in life that *did* still hold such promise.

So I didn't prepare a single job application. When my colleagues asked about my plans after the end of my fellowship, I told them I was going to farm and write. I admit that when I thought about the number of decisions that had to be made in order to create this new life—and the amount of money needed to make them—my confidence sometimes wavered. When my colleagues asked where this farm was going to be, I had to say that I didn't know for sure, not even about the continent. But, whenever I worried that I was nothing but a foolish dreamer, I picked up one of Wendell Berry's books. And I quickly got back my determination to live the life I knew in my heart I was meant for. A life of unrelenting independence.

Maybe that's why I'd brought *Wendell Berry: Life and Work* along to the coffee shop. I was feeling worried again. Things had been coming together so perfectly over the summer. Samuel's dad had told us he would give us the farm, and I had been able to meet a couple of people in the French publishing industry. It was like everything I'd needed for the realization of my dreams had been offered to me on a silver platter. And then it had been unceremoniously yanked back. I felt lost. What kind of dreams could I have now that everything I'd previously hung them on was in jeopardy?

I hopefully opened to the first page of *Wendell Berry: Life and Work*. The introduction, written by Jason Peters, began by comparing Wendell Berry to Henry David Thoreau. Reflecting on this, I was surprised to realize that I had discovered both of these authors within the same stretch of two or three months in the summer of 2008, right after my graduation from NYU. Samuel had given me a French translation of *Walden* for my twenty-seventh birthday, which happened to be the very day that he and I traveled to Waltham to look for our apartment. In a brilliant coincidence, on that very same day, Samuel and I realized that Thoreau's Walden Pond was located in Concord, Massachusetts, just ten miles west of Waltham.

I began reading *Walden* that very day, and came upon the passage in which Thoreau's friend suggests to him that he take the train from Concord to Fitchburg to see the sights. Thoreau scoffs at the idea. Why would he spend a day's pay on a train ticket when he could just walk? Instead of spending ten hours laboring in Concord and then being rushed off to Fitchburg at nightfall, he could spend the entire day walking through the countryside!

I loved this mindset, and even though Samuel and I were on a schedule that didn't allow us to walk all the way from Boston to Waltham, once we'd gotten to Waltham, we *did* do all our apartment hunting on foot. And how did we get there, without stooping to renting a car? By riding the very train line that Thoreau had referred to one hundred fifty years before, which still had Fitchburg listed as its final stop!

Jason Peters' essay comparing Berry and Thoreau brought together two crucial threads of my life. It was like a summary of the most important developments in my ideas over the two years that Samuel and I had been living in Waltham. On the second page, Peters wrote, "Neither Thoreau nor Berry suffers damage by the comparison. One went to the woods to live deliberately; the other went home to live defensibly." *That's right*, I thought. *Berry went home.*

There I was, forced by circumstance back to my parents' house, back to the county where I'd grown up, back to the town that contained the hospital where I'd been born. And I'd been feeling embarrassed about it. Sad. Defeated. Maybe because all my plans for my life had always included going somewhere else. As a child, I'd thought God was calling me to be a missionary to China. In college, I'd thought Daniel and I were going to be economic development workers in Ecuador. More recently, I'd been expecting to live in Brittany. Naturally, I would view my forced return home as a failure.

But I realized that that wasn't the only way to look at it. What if, like Wendell Berry, I was actually *meant* to come home? Berry, by his writing, had immortalized his rural county in Kentucky. What if I was meant, in my writing, to immortalize the corner of the U.S. where *I* lived?

I knew it was a bit grandiose to imagine myself as Virginia's Wendell Berry. It was a goal every bit as difficult to attain as that of becoming a world-renowned philosopher. But the vision of it thrilled me in a way I had never been thrilled by imagining myself as a prestigious academic. Even when I'd received the NYU Dean's Dissertation Award, or had an article published in a top philosophy journal, I was pleased, certainly, but I didn't feel any deep sense of accomplishment. It was more the feeling of having done something *other* people admired. But when I imagined publishing novels and memoirs about life in Massachusetts or Virginia…*that* felt like greatness.

Suddenly, less than three pages into my book on Wendell Berry, I felt inspired with an idea for an essay of my own. I took out a sheet of loose-leaf paper I'd tucked into my bag. "Some people call the part of town where I live 'tow-truck' Waltham," I wrote at the top. Then I went on to describe all the things about that part of Waltham that some people might view as unsightly, and definitely not utopian: the long parade of garages and auto body repair shops with their streams of oil and gasoline trickling out into the street, the yard circled by a mangled chain-link fence that was left to grow up in weeds and small trees, the overflowing garbage cans behind the fast food restaurant around which a crowd of seagulls always hovered, and the sidewalks that the New England winters had heaved up into minor mountain ranges. "The tow trucks keep away people who might want things too *clean*," I wrote. "Waltham is alive because the human domination of it is incomplete. There are edges and seams where a more complex, vibrant, and varied world peeks through."

It was a very short essay, only two handwritten pages. And it wasn't brilliant. But I was describing my personal experience of utopia, trying to convey the perfection I saw in those neglected stretches of pavement in southwest Waltham. And writing it felt like opening a door to the future. Like getting a peek at the sorts of things I would be thinking and writing about for years to come.*

When I drove home that afternoon, over the Rappahannock River and east past acre after acre of corn stubble, I felt like I had truly accomplished something. I hadn't just managed to spend three hours thinking about something other than when Samuel would come back to me. I had dreamed a new dream. The essay in my ENS satchel gave me hope. A hope that did not depend on Samuel.

Unfortunately, when I stepped through the door of my parents' house, I could feel my sense of triumph and independence flee and the worries resettle on my shoulders. Back in my room, sitting on my worn homemade quilt, I was just the same old Sharon. I looked at Samuel's picture, and I no longer felt like someone who could take on the world. I just wanted to curl up in the arms of the man I loved. Wanted, for a few moments, not to have to be strong. Not to have to take care of myself. I wanted someone *else* to do the sacrificing and the hard work.

Would that be possible? I wondered. *Just this once?*

The next morning, I had another email from Samuel.

"I hate the idea," he said, "but I feel like my life is carrying me away from you."

---

* That essay was eventually published in the November/December 2014 issue of *Orion* magazine, Vol. 33, No. 5, pp. 8-9.

Chapter EIGHT

None of it made any sense. Only a week and a half ago, Samuel had told me he was feeling more confident about the wedding. How could he now say that his life was carrying him away from me? And say it in a way that refused to acknowledge his own responsibility in the matter? People's lives didn't just carry them away from the people they loved. They made a conscious choice to be led away. This girl, whoever she was, couldn't have any power over Samuel that he hadn't granted her. So why was he going so willingly?

Sometime in the last couple of weeks, in an effort to explain the hold she had on him, Samuel had pointed out that he had known her for fifteen years. *So?* I wanted to shout. *We've known each other for nine. And we've been living together for the last two. You've never even kissed this girl!* That is, if I could believe what he'd told me. And I still believed I could.

I had been trying so hard to understand. So hard to see what it was that Samuel was going through. What kind of issues his seeing this girl from his past had reawakened in him and what might be done to resolve them. But now it seemed like Samuel was just giving up. Without a fight. Without even acknowledging that he was making a *choice*.

I suddenly hit the bottom of my well of patience. If Samuel thought that the issue was settled, that his life was "carrying him away from me," then I was certainly not going to waste any more of my precious energy holding us together. This was an ending that I had not foreseen and which made absolutely no sense to me, but if this was how things had to be, then I just wanted the nightmare of waiting and wondering to be over.

I replied to Samuel's email with a list of things I had left in Brittany: my pressure cooker, my Region 2 DVDs, my copy of Joel Salatin's *Pastured Poultry Profits*. "Please mail them to me at my parents' house," I told him.

It was about eight o'clock in the morning. I went down to the basement and found my mom stretched out on a yoga mat in front of the TV. "Things with Samuel are over," I told her, in a surprisingly even voice.

She gave me a sympathetic look. "Do you want to go for a walk?"

I shrugged. "Sure."

It was another beautiful September day. We walked down my parents' subdivision street, past homes whose well-trimmed yards and spotless flower borders seemed to reflect the wonderfully settled nature of everyone else's life. "I guess it's like you said," I told Mom. "I'm going to have a hard time finding a husband."

"What? I said that?"

"When I was a teenager." I was pretty sure she'd meant it as a compliment. That I was going to have a hard time finding someone who was my equal.

"Well," she said, "don't think about that right now."

But, after two failed engagements, it was a little hard not to. How could I not feel that I was doing something wrong? Perhaps, with all my utopianism, I was too demanding. *Trop exigeante*, as the French say. Maybe I wasn't enough fun. Or beautiful enough. Maybe I should wear fewer plaid shirts. Or more make up? As strong as my self-esteem had always been—as much as I'd prided myself on scoffing at others' opinions and beating my own path through life—I couldn't completely silence the doubting voice inside me, the one that said there *must* be something wrong with me, if the man who knew me better and loved me more than anyone else in the world was nevertheless capable of leaving me for someone else.

When my mom and I got back to the house, I realized there was no way I could settle in for another day there, sewing and reading and listening to this voice inside my head. I desperately needed a change of scenery. After weighing my options, I decided to visit my sister Rebecca. She and her husband Ryan were in seminary at Wake Forest University in North Carolina, about five hours away. I had always gotten along well with both of them. They were religious—they were both studying to become pastors—but they were also very open-minded and humble. I never felt like they looked down on me because I was an atheist. And they were not in thrall to any moralistic dogma.

When I'd flown to Paris for Christmas break the year before Samuel and I got together, Rebecca and Ryan were both studying at the University of St Andrew's in Scotland, and they came down to meet me for a couple of days. They stayed over in the apartment I'd been lent, and even though they weren't married yet—they'd only just gotten engaged—they slept in the same bed. It was something my parents would never have allowed if they'd been around. But we were thousands of miles away from our parents, and I remember feeling a deep kinship with Rebecca and Ryan over their willingness to make their own choices—a feeling like, "Here are two other people in this family who are willing to be a little different. For the sake of following their own hearts."

When Samuel and I got together, Rebecca and Ryan became good friends with Samuel—Ryan in particular—and I never felt the least bit of judgment from them with regard to our living together unmarried. I figured that, if I could tell the whole story to anyone, it would be to them.

My mom loaned me her car for the trip. Steve Tyrell was in the CD player, and as I drove along I-95 through the center of Richmond, I listened to him sing "Give Me the Simple Life." It was hard for me to imagine the simple life without Samuel. It was the kind of life I'd been hankering after since high school, when I planted my first, extremely weedy vegetable garden and spent hot summer afternoons reading about building outhouses and skinning rabbits. But it was only when I found Samuel that I had my first true experience of farm life, in his backyard in Brittany. And I had trouble now, imagining the fulfillment of that dream in his absence. I *wanted* to imagine finding someone else to share it with, someone who was just as good for me as Samuel had been. But it quite frankly seemed impossible. Already, my relationship with Samuel had been almost too good to be true. The way he understood and affirmed every part of me: my intellectual side, my Christian side, my atheist side, my French side, my American side, my city side, my country side. It wasn't realistic to expect *two* such relationships in one lifetime. To find another man whose puzzle pieces meshed so precisely with mine? It just wasn't going to happen.

But as I listened to Tyrell's cheerful simple-life manifesto, I urged myself to forget the daunting odds. Told myself there was no harm in fantasizing a little, to take the edge off the pain. I tried thinking about all the little things Samuel did that irked me, and about finding someone who didn't have those traits. Someone, for instance, who would come to dinner right when I called, not after he finished the next ten pages of his book. Someone who would not just accept that *I* wanted to have a farm and maybe build my own house but someone who would enjoy helping me do those things. Someone who would join me in plucking chickens without complaining. Or willingly take a tour of my vegetable garden. Most of all, someone who would never leave me behind.

In fact, I did much better at filling out the fantasy than I anticipated. The only problem was that it lacked the one thing I wanted more than anything else: Samuel himself. With all his shortcomings, he was the one I desired. My longing was for *him*, and the best imaginary lover in the world couldn't take that longing away.

When I got to Rebecca's late that afternoon, I plopped down on her couch and told her and Ryan the whole story, including the real reason behind Samuel's change of heart. Now that my relationship with Samuel was officially at an end, I no longer had to save face for him. I didn't have to hedge my bets, worrying about whether the things I said would make people disapprove if we ultimately got back together. And, without the energy drain of worrying about what decision Samuel was going to make, I finally felt strong enough to deal with any associated embarrassment.

But in fact I *didn't* feel embarrassed when I told Rebecca and Ryan that Samuel was leaving me for another woman. And I didn't cry, either. Or even get choked up. Rebecca and Ryan were shocked and sad, but I actually felt proud of myself for being able to relate everything so matter-of-factly. "At least I'm not in a state of uncertainty anymore," I said. "At least things are clear." It certainly didn't feel *good* to be announcing the end of my relationship with the man I loved, but having clarity put me in a better place than I had been for the last few weeks. Any clarity, good or bad, was a place to start. A foundation on which to build my recovery.

Sitting in Rebecca and Ryan's university apartment, eating dinner at their carefully laid dining table, sipping red wine from the stemless goblets they'd received as wedding presents, I felt almost normal. Even if seeing their wedding presents did remind me of Samuel's first visit to my parents' home. Rebecca and Ryan had gotten married just a month after Samuel and I began dating, and Samuel had needed no persuading to seize the opportunity to come to the States. He'd joined in the preparations and the celebration as if he were already a member of the family. My mind filled with memories of Samuel at the wedding—leading me onto the dance floor, chatting in French with my Aunt Claire, discussing religion with one of Rebecca's friends who was an ex-Catholic—but I managed to keep my emotions at bay. I managed to return my focus to the present. Here in Rebecca and Ryan's apartment, I had the chance to make the first memories of my future life. The one without Samuel.

After dinner, Ryan decided to put on some music. For Christmas the previous year, Rebecca and Ryan had given me an album by David Gray, an English singer-songwriter I hadn't heard of. The album didn't do much for me when I first listened to it—maybe at the time I was too happy to appreciate his somber melodies?—but when I came back from France the following summer and received Samuel's startling news, Gray's voice suddenly became a lifeline. The worst period of every twenty-four hours was the time when I lay down to sleep. In those dark, quiet moments, the grief threatened to become unbearable. To soothe myself into unconsciousness, I pulled my boom box over next to the bed and put *White Ladder* on repeat. Gray's resonant, slightly nasal voice—like a more melodious version of Bob Dylan—sang me my lullaby.

Knowing nothing about my associations with David Gray, Ryan now put one of his songs on the living room stereo. And, as I heard Gray's voice fill the apartment, my chest began to heave with the same grief I'd spent the last month using him to keep at bay. Still sitting at the dining table, I covered my face with my hands and said quietly to Ryan, "I'm sorry. Can we turn that off?"

A little while later, Rebecca and Ryan made me a bed in their spare room: a blow-up mattress covered in blankets and throws. I nestled in, and despite the lack of music to which to fall asleep, I slept surprisingly well. I didn't wake up until the dawn light began creeping through the blinds around 6:30. I lay there for a while, gathering my energy for the day, wondering what I would find to occupy myself. Maybe I would try the campus coffee shop. I had *Wendell Berry: Life and Work* in my suitcase. Or I could make a trip to the university library. Borrow some DVDs to watch with Rebecca when she got out of class.

As I was lying there contemplating the day's possibilities, my phone rang. I fetched it from where it was charging on top of Ryan's desk and saw that the number began with 33—the country code for France. "*Allô?*" I said, in my scratchy morning voice.

"*Shahone.*"

I hadn't heard Samuel's voice in so long. Its deep tenderness brought tears to my eyes. "Hey," I said.

"Do you really want me to send you your things, or were you just being provocative?"

What did he mean, was I being provocative? *He* was the one who'd said his life was carrying him away from me. "It sounded from your email like things were clearly over between us," I said. "I think we need to move on."

"*Shahone!*" he moaned. "Please."

"Please what?"

"It's not like that. I *love* you. I want to be with you."

"Well, then be with me. What's the problem?"

He didn't say anything for a long moment. "The problem is…I can't."

"Why not?"

He sighed. "You're going to think I'm crazy."

"No, I won't," I told him. Even if part of me already did.

"I don't know if I can say it," he hedged. Then finally he came out with it: "I think God wants me to do something else."

Oh, sure, Samuel. Real mature. Blame it on God.

I probably should have been more sympathetic. It hadn't been that long ago that I'd had similar thoughts about God. When I was a teenager, I'd identified the voice of God not by its compassion or its incredibly good sense, but by the fear it struck into my heart. If I recoiled at the thought of doing something, my adolescent mind immediately thought God *must* be calling me to do it—whether it was risking my life smuggling Bibles into Communist China or approaching a big tatted-up guy in McDonald's and asking if he wanted to accept Jesus into his heart.

But that was over ten years ago. I'd long ago outgrown that masochistic conception of God. And replaced it with a burgeoning faith in my own judgment. Shouldn't Samuel, at thirty-three years old, have also been past the stage of thinking God always wanted him to do what he didn't want to do? After all, half the time Samuel claimed God didn't even exist.

Nevertheless, I had a strong hunch about what Samuel thought God wanted him to do. He'd never said as much, but deep down I felt there was only one thing that could have pulled him so quickly and forcefully away from me. "Do you think God wants you to marry *her*?" I asked.

There were several torturous seconds during which he didn't reply. Several very telling seconds. I sighed, my chest heavy with this new level of clarity.

"I think I *do* have to be with her," Samuel said finally, dropping the God language. "I can't explain it...but that doesn't mean I don't love you. I do. You'll never know how much I love you, Sharon."

No, I guess I never will. If you loved me that much, I doubt you'd be leaving me for someone else. Or even thinking God was asking you to.

But even though Samuel's thought processes seemed confused and his theological beliefs less than rational, in the end it didn't really matter. Because I knew that, ultimately, this wasn't a question of the mind. It was a question of the heart. And it was becoming clear that Samuel's heart was not fully—or even mostly—mine.

"I love you, too," I told him. "And I want you to be happy. If that means you have to be with her, then that's what you have to do."

"It's not about being happy, Sharon. My life isn't about happiness."

For some reason, this statement of his angered me more than any of the others. I'd spent all my life looking for the kind of happiness I had finally found with Samuel. How could he now say that happiness was *irrelevant* to the decision he was making? "What the hell else is your life about?!" I wanted to shout.

"With you, I've been happier than at any other time in my life," Samuel went on. "You've made me happier than I ever will be again. But there's something else that's calling me now."

This was sounding really crazy. I mean, Samuel had always had a slightly different vision of life from the people around him. He'd always been very little concerned with material things. Even with eating. Or drinking anything other than coffee, the fuel for his writing. He was impatient whenever family obligations—or even his obligations to me—got in the way of time at his computer. "I wish I was a monk," he'd say in those moments.

"Oh, that makes me feel really great," I'd respond.

"You know what I mean."

But I wasn't sure I did. Since Samuel clearly enjoyed being with me, I assumed he just meant he wanted fewer day-to-day distractions, and the ability to single-mindedly concentrate on whatever book he was currently writing. I could certainly identify with that. But now I wondered if Samuel thought he was called to be a monk because it would mean being sad and lonely, and he believed that was what he deserved. Or was fated for, somehow.

It worried me that Samuel saw this enormous choice in his life as coming from outside himself, as being at crossed purposes with his own desires. "I love you. I want to be with you," he had told me. "But God wants me to do something else." Part of me hoped that, deep down, he actually *wanted* to be with this other girl and was just too polite to tell me. I would feel less worried for him then.

"I'm so sorry," he said to me now, over the phone. "I never, ever want to hurt you."

"I know," I replied. The only person Samuel seemed to *want* to hurt was himself. And apparently, as hard as I was trying, that was not something I could save him from. "At least we can separate with understanding," I said, "not anger. We can be together even as we're parting."

"Yes, I would like that."

We stayed quiet for a long while, neither of us wanting to hang up the phone but neither of us knowing what else to say. The silence grew, but it wasn't uncomfortable. In fact, it was a moment of deep intimacy. In being able to accept Samuel's decision—to offer him gentleness and understanding even in these incredibly trying circumstances—I felt closer to him than ever before.

Finally, Samuel broke the silence. "I want to say something stupid," he said.

"Go ahead."

"No. Never mind."

I hated when he did that, but I was done trying to pull the truth out of him. At least the essential things had been said. "Well," I said, "I guess this is goodbye."

"We're not going to talk again?" asked Samuel.

"Well, probably not." Wasn't that the idea? God wanted him to marry someone else. What else did we have to talk about?

"I love you, Sharon."

"I love you, too, Samuel. And I wish you every wonderful thing. I hope that you *do* find happiness, in spite of yourself."

"I wish you all wonderful things, too. I wish that you find the life you are intended for. And I want you to know I will always think of you. I will *always* love you. You are my angel. My gift from God. What we have is something that can never be replaced."

I nodded, even if he couldn't see me. "I love you, Samuel."

"I love you more than you will ever know, *Shahone.*"

Part of me could have stayed on the phone forever listening to him say such things. Piling these little gems up in my heart. These glistening sentimental treasures, unearthed only after our plunge into the deep, disorienting mineshafts of the human heart. And yet, as beautiful as Samuel's sentiments were, I had been clearly informed that none of them would spare us the coming separation. And, at some point, we had to move on into that future.

So what was the right way to say goodbye? Normally, French people said, "*Au revoir.*" But that literally meant "until the next time we see each other." That not only seemed inaccurate in this case, it also felt much too ordinary. Unequal to the gravity of the situation. A better choice, I thought, was "*Adieu.*" It was a more permanent goodbye, and it literally meant, "to God."

So I said it. "*Adieu, Samuel.*" And, as I spoke the words, I hoped that there was a God. And that that God would be a trustworthy caretaker for Samuel's soul.

"Goodbye, Shahone," he said, in English.

We hung up.

I was proud of myself for being strong enough to behave lovingly toward Samuel even when the situation was so difficult. This was the most unconditional love I could think of. To love even when your love was not returned. Even when the object of your love was turning his gaze elsewhere.

But this pride did little to mitigate the pain of the loss. For the next three days, several times a day, the suffering became so acute that it felt like someone had a pair of pliers clamped around my heart, with the goal of ripping it out like a rotten tooth. In this state of suffering, the Wake Forest University library no longer held any attraction for me. Nor did the Starbucks just outside the entrance. When I could push myself to get off Rebecca's couch, I wandered the wooded trails that snaked around the campus. But the beauty of the lofty oaks and poplars only made me more despairing. I felt incapable of appreciating them, incapable of being distracted from my grief. I stood for a long time beside a brook where it rippled across a bed of pebbles. I wanted its gurgling to lift my sadness. But instead we just sat there, the three of us: the brook, my sadness, and me.

One afternoon, the sky was heavy with rain clouds. As they grew darker and thicker, I turned my steps back toward my sister's apartment and picked up my pace. When I got within a few hundred yards, I ran—across the lawn and down the steps to the sunken patio beside her basement door. And as soon as I crossed the threshold, it began to pour.

No one else was home. I opened the blinds and watched from the window as a river of water gushed down the steps of the patio and swirled into the drain. The rain reminded me of a time Samuel and I had made love to an afternoon thunderstorm. We'd been in Brittany, and we'd both taken a break from our reading and writing for a little nap. Then, as our nap turned into something a bit more vigorous, the weather did, too. The wind picked up, slashing rain against the window of Samuel's bedroom and causing the wooden shutters to tremble violently in their brackets. Lightning flashed across the room, with the thunder roaring in close behind. It was as if the natural world was caught up in our passion—intensifying and electrifying it. And then suddenly, just as that passion was reaching its peak, from somewhere inside the house, we heard a tremendous *CRACK*. We looked at each other, eyes wide. *What the...?* We threw on our clothes and rushed downstairs to find that the TV had been blown out.

Thinking of the crazy magic of that summer afternoon made my heart ache all the more. Where before I had been just barely able to contain the sadness, now it tore at me insistently. Urgently. *Do something*, it demanded. *Find the man you love!* I pulled Rebecca's laptop from its spot under the coffee table. It had been three days since I'd had any communication with Samuel. Now I wrote him a very short email: "It's raining here. I miss you terribly." I hit "send," then lay back against the couch cushions.

For a few moments, I watched the rain continue to fall. And in one of those strange shifts of perception—like when the hidden image in a Magic Eye poster finally jumps out at you—it suddenly felt to me as though the drops of rain racing down the window pane were the tears of God, crying along with me. Crying a river of tears longer and wider than my slight human frame could ever produce.

But even as I felt the odd sense that God was weeping with me, I didn't understand how that could be true. If there was a God, how could that God ever allow such a tragic dismantling of my life? A ripping of emotional limb from emotional limb? If once I had wanted to believe in a good universe, where everything happened for a good reason, that option did not feel open to me now. What I had known with Samuel was *too* good. Too good for *anything* to justify yanking it away. I was convinced, in the ever-tightening clutches of my despair, that a good God would never have allowed this sort of pain into the world.

While I was still thinking these thoughts, a reply from Samuel appeared in my inbox. "I'm here," he wrote. "It's raining in Brittany, too."

I could feel the relief of his presence physically spread through my bloodstream, starting in my head, heart, and lungs, and then flowing down my arms and legs. It was as though Samuel was for me a literal drug, and I'd been in withdrawal for the past three days. Two little sentences from him and every tension, every worry, every negative emotion was instantly banished by the cool euphoria racing through my veins.

"If we were together on a day like this," I wrote back, "I would make love to you."

Again, Samuel replied almost instantly. "That's what I wanted to say on the phone," he wrote. "I wanted to tell you to come to France so we could make love again. But I didn't want to make things worse."

"I'm making love to you right now," I replied.

"Yes," he said. "I'm making love to you, too."

I continued to sit on the couch and watch the rain, and I thought about having Samuel in my arms. *Just give me this moment*, I said, to no one in particular. *Just this one brief moment of rest.*

Samuel and I emailed back and forth for forty-five minutes. Just small talk. Just saying how much we missed each other. Then Rebecca came home, and I needed to help her make dinner. "Can we talk again tomorrow?" I asked Samuel.

"Yes," he said. "Whenever you want."

We met on Instant Messenger at nine the next morning. Rebecca had taken her laptop to class, so I went to the Wake Forest library to use a public computer. As soon as I signed on, Samuel told me he had a story to tell. About a coincidence that had happened to him just a few hours ago. "I was at my grandmother's helping install her new stove," he wrote. "And when I went to set the clock, I asked Tante Monique what time it was. She said, '11:32. No, wait. 11:33.'"

Samuel had turned thirty-three years old the previous February. Soon after his birthday, he had told me that he expected this to be a crucial year in his life. "Jesus was crucified at thirty-three," he said, by way of explanation. And though I wasn't quite sure what to make of that comparison, it did go along with Samuel's feeling that he had an unhappy destiny.

From that time on, he started seeing the number thirty-three everywhere. He was always pointing it out in newspaper headlines: thirty-three workers were trapped in a mine in Bolivia, the Miss France Pageant had thirty-three contestants. "You're just seeing 33s now because you're more attentive to them," I told him. And when he would interrupt my reading to tell me, once again, that he had just looked at the clock and it was thirty-three minutes past the hour, I would shake my head and reassure him, *"Ça arrive vingt-quatre fois par jour!"* That happens twenty-four times a day!

But his story with the stove got a little more interesting. After his Aunt Monique announced the time as thirty-three minutes past the hour, Samuel started rotating the dial on the clock, and his uncle—

who knew nothing about Samuel's obsession with 33s, nor anything about the recent upheaval in his personal life—immediately exclaimed, "Watch out! At thirty-three, it explodes!"

I chuckled in the middle of the library stacks. Samuel's life did indeed seem to have exploded. At the same time, I couldn't help wishing that Samuel would find a coincidence that would tell him something more positive. For instance, a coincidence that would tell him that things were going to work out between us.

Samuel and I chatted for an hour and a half that morning. When we signed off, it was only after agreeing to meet again at two that afternoon. Then, that afternoon, we made a date to meet again the next morning. And the next morning, we agreed to meet again *that* afternoon.

On the evening after our third day of this new round of communication, I was sitting alone in Rebecca's living room, curled up in her overstuffed chair. It was 8pm in the States. Two in the morning in France. Samuel had long since gone to bed, and even though we had talked just hours before, I was nevertheless feeling his absence. To fill the void, I pulled out Rebecca's computer and read an email that my friend Debbie had sent to cheer me up. When I closed that window, I saw I had a new email from Samuel.

It contained just three precious words: "I miss you."

"Me, too," I immediately wrote back.

A few seconds later, he followed up with another email. "Look at this video I just found," he wrote. Attached was a link to a U2 concert video, in which they performed a new song of theirs called "Glastonbury."

Just a month and a half before, Samuel and I had visited the town of Glastonbury in England. It had been one of the highlights of our engagement trip to the UK. We'd planned on going there because Samuel was fascinated with the Arthurian legends, and King Arthur had supposedly been buried in Glastonbury Abbey. But what had stuck with me most was our trip to the top of Glastonbury Tor.

Glastonbury Tor was just outside of the town: an enormous hill rising incongruously from the surrounding plain. Despite the wind that whistled around it—so strong that it gave me an earache—Samuel and I climbed the sinuous, boulder-strewn path all the way to its peak. In the fourteenth century, the Church of St Michael had apparently been built there, at the very top. Nothing remained of it now save a roofless, windswept tower, and the wind seemed violent enough to one day bear that away as well. But somehow that seemed appropriate. The Tor didn't need to be crowned by a church. The inhabitants of this land had revered it as a holy site long before the Christians came along. And standing there at the top, I understood why.

With our backs to the stone tower, Samuel and I looked out over the surrounding flatlands, dotted with sheep and patches of mist. I don't know if it was the vastness of the view or the biting wind or something else altogether, but I found as I looked down on the lush countryside from such a height that I felt no attraction at all to my usual atheistic, mechanistic view of the universe. As I stood atop the Tor, something fiercely mystical rose in my chest. I suppose you could call it awe. A recognition of a power and grandeur independent of the work of human hands. It momentarily convinced me of the truth of that line from Hamlet: "There are more things in heaven and earth, Horatio, Than are dreamt of in your philosophy."

"First U2 followed us to Morocco," wrote Samuel in his email. "Now to Glastonbury."

He and I watched the video together, each on our own side of the Atlantic. Bono's lyrics were all about pilgrimage, and about releasing one's hold on the things one can't control in life. After the Glastonbury video, Samuel and I watched other clips from the same concert. We'd send each other the links and watch them at the same time. In sync across four thousand miles.

"I feel at peace," I wrote to him, when we finally prepared to sign off and go to bed.

"Me, too," he said. "Peace."

As I drifted off to sleep that night, I wondered whether all our recent communication was the sign of a turnaround. We seemed to be so close to one another now, and in such need of each other. After all, it was Samuel who had written to *me* at two in the morning. And there had been no sign in any of our internet conversations of Samuel's previous statement that his life was carrying him away from me. He was more present than he'd been at any point in the past month. Maybe he was realizing that that statement had been a mistake—an expression of his fears, not of his deepest heart.

The next morning, I started the drive home to my parents'. I would have been happy to stay longer with Rebecca and Ryan, but my mom needed her car back. And it seemed like it was time. Time to embark on the next leg of this journey, whatever that might be.

The drive started out thoroughly ordinary. It was a warm, sunny day. In fact, in North Carolina, you could hardly tell that summer had become fall. It was early October, but everything was still as green and vibrant as ever. And I was feeling pretty vibrant and sunny myself. I hummed as I drove along I-85 toward Virginia.

A little before lunchtime, I pulled into a rest stop. As I pulled up in front of the brick building, the first thing that caught my eye was the name of the town, spelled out in metal letters attached to the brick wall. "Granville, NC," it said. Granville, it happened, was the name of the town in Normandy where Samuel and I had gone on our very first weekend together as a couple.

It was the weekend of the 2007 French presidential election. Samuel had to go back home to vote and invited me along. To protect our infant relationship from prying questions—we'd had our first kiss only the night before—Samuel told his family I was coming with him because I was interested in "seeing the French electoral process." I think Samuel's dad guessed the truth, even before he saw Samuel sneaking out of my bedroom at 7am. But still we pretended to be only friends, and just smiled knowingly at each other when we heard the words to the Gérald De Palmas song Samuel put on in the living room, "*Elle Habite Ici*": *She lives here…she sleeps in my bed.…* To hug and kiss in freedom, we snuck away from the family for an afternoon, to the seaside town of Granville, Normandy.

It was cold and windy that early May day. I wore a windbreaker and huddled close to Samuel's side as we walked the cliffs above the sea. When we found our way down to the beach, the wind was much less strong, so we took off our shoes and socks and walked barefoot in the sand. "I think you were right about my being like Nancy Huston," I told Samuel. "I think I'm ready to be a writer."

"You *are* a writer," he said.

"Maybe." I thought about the spiritual memoir I'd been trying for years to compose. I had racked up a hundred pages or so, but I hated the tone of it. It sounded so self-consciously clever. "I think there's still a lot of work I have to do. But what I mean is, I'm starting to see myself not just as someone who writes, but as a writer. Someone who can't live *without* writing."

"I think you're *exactly* like Nancy Huston," he said, squeezing my hand.

A month later, for my birthday, he gave me an autographed copy of Nancy Huston's book *Désirs et Réalités*. He'd come across her at a book fair in Saint-Malo, and he'd had her inscribe the title page for me: "These desires and realities are for Sharon with the friendship of Nancy Huston."

All these memories were in my mind as I parked the car in front of the rest stop building in Granville, North Carolina. Full of nostalgia, I turned off the car and glanced down at the dash. The clock read 12:33.

Now, as I'd frequently told Samuel, a clock reads "33" twenty-four times a day. There is one chance in sixty that, when you look at a clock, it will say "33." So it wasn't exactly a miracle. And yet, for me, there was something startling about seeing a 33 at precisely that moment. Because of the mindset I'd been in when I saw it—already affected by the coincidence of a rest stop named Granville—it caught my attention in a way none of Samuel's coincidences ever had.

A little later, back on the road, I noticed that the last exit in North Carolina was Exit 233. And that it was for a town named Wise. It was exactly the kind of thing Samuel would have pointed out. "Wisdom is exactly what we need," he would have said.

Once I was back on the Virginia side of the line, I stopped for gas. And then, not long after that, I got hungry for lunch, so I pulled off the interstate at a Wendy's. When I stopped the car this time, the trip mileage, which I had reset when I filled up the gas tank, now read exactly 33.

An hour or so later, I passed a self-storage facility whose phone number was printed in large numbers on its sign: 633-3333. And ten minutes after that, I had to make my first turn in half an hour. The mile marker at the turn was 133. And then I turned onto my parents' street, noticing for the first time that its county route number ended in 33.

It was a lot of coincidences. But I was convinced they were just that: coincidences. Even if I were willing to consider that there might be something out of the ordinary going on, what would that even be? What meaning could a string of 33s possibly have? I had no idea.

Once back at my parents' house, I kept messaging Samuel a couple of times a day. Our new degree of connection kept my suffering at bay, and I felt generally level-headed and sane. I also felt that, maybe, if we could hold onto this connection long enough, Samuel would have time to come around. We talked about all sorts of things besides the future.

A week later, my parents took me on a two-day excursion to the mountains. The idea was to drive down Skyline Drive, stopping at all the overlooks, and then stay in a fancy hotel near Charlottesville. My mom thought it would help me take my mind off things. But in fact I was pretty depressed at the thought of spending an entire weekend without any IM conversations with Samuel. I could have taken my laptop to the hotel, but it was seven years old and couldn't connect to any Wi-Fi networks that didn't have passwords exactly ten characters long, so there was hardly any point.

As my parents and I drove west toward the mountains, I sat in the back seat of the car thinking lonely thoughts. Mom was poring over the road atlas, questioning Dad about our route. When we were about halfway there, she asked him, "What's the next turn?"

"The next turn," he said, "is onto the road that'll take us the rest of the way there. Route 33."

Route 33. The road that'll take us the rest of the way there. I wished with every wishing bone of my body for this to be a message from the universe—a message that Samuel and I were nearing the end of this long ordeal.

That night, Mom and Dad and I got dressed up and went out to an expensive restaurant, where I ordered coriander-crusted ahi tuna followed by roasted sweet potato and goat cheese faro with broken pistachio vinaigrette. Just as we were finishing our first course, I saw several men in tuxedoes enter the dining room, escorting ladies in matching evening gowns. I knew what was bound to follow, and it gave me a knot in the pit of my stomach. Sure enough, a few moments later, a beaming bride and groom appeared. While they settled themselves in their private banquet room, I looked into the remains of my tuna and willed myself not to cry.

"How's your fish?" asked my dad.

"I'm sorry," I said. "I have to go to the bathroom."

Once tucked safely into a stall, I braced myself against the back of the door and gave myself a long, thorough cry. Thankfully, I only had to take one more sob break before dinner was over. After that, I held myself off with thoughts of the private hotel room my parents had thoughtfully reserved for me. *After dinner,* I told myself, *you can cry all you want in privacy.*

But, when I walked into the hotel room fifteen minutes later, I found I couldn't stay. Maybe it was the fact that the last time I'd been in a hotel was at Atlantic Beach, the night of Samuel's fateful telephone call. In any case, being alone was not the comfort I'd expected.

So I went next door, where my parents were both outfitted in their hotel robes, reading. Dad was in a wingback chair, and Mom was sitting on one end of a tiny sofa. Without a word, I curled up next to her and put my head in her lap. I lay there with my cheek pressed against the terrycloth, soaking it with my tears as she gently stroked my hair.

I thought about a conversation I'd had with her the previous year, about my sleeping with Samuel. "Sex bonds you so much to someone," she'd said, trying to explain why she thought we shouldn't have slept together before we were married. "If you break up, it makes it almost like a divorce."

"We're not going to break up," I told her. "But if we did, it would be painful even if we'd never had sex. Because we love each other. *That's* what makes the bond between us. I love him so much it would feel like a divorce even if we had never made love."

And I still believed that was true.

But I wondered what my mom was thinking now, with me crying in her lap. Was she saying to herself, *If only you hadn't slept with him, it wouldn't hurt so much?* If those were her thoughts, it didn't show. She continued to gently touch my hair and didn't say a word.

The next day, the three of us were sitting around the hotel room again, and I started looking through a binder about the amenities available. I found descriptions of the massages offered in the hotel spa. The "Stone Therapy" sounded particularly good. It featured warm and cool basalt and marble stones, strategically placed to release tension and stress.

"Why don't you get a massage?" asked my mom, when she saw what I was reading. "We'll pay for it."

"That's okay," I said. "Just reading the descriptions is relaxing." And it was. The words alone had a deeply soothing effect. There was another treatment that featured oregano, wintergreen, and other essential oils dripped along the spine like raindrops, followed by massage and a hot towel application. My muscles tingled as I read the description. My whole body felt warmer, like it was being very gently cared for. And I knew that that was one of the things I needed to do: take care of myself. And not rely on Samuel or anyone else to do it for me.

When I got home, Samuel and I picked back up our online conversations as if we'd never stopped. But even as they continued over the course of the next several days, they didn't seem to be having the effect I'd been hoping for. On the rare occasions when the future came up, Samuel still seemed lost. "I don't know," was his most common reply to my questions. So it was all happening all over again. We were right back in the same miasma of uncertainty.

And I just didn't understand it. I didn't understand why our new closeness wasn't enough to convince Samuel that we were supposed to be together. *Look at everything we've been through!* I wanted to say. *Look how strong our love still is! What could we possibly not handle together?* But our conversations didn't appear to be making him any more confident about the way forward.

It had been a month and a half since Samuel had first announced he couldn't marry me, and I again started to wonder if it was ever going to get better. If he was still feeling so conflicted—after all of this proof that we were so good for each other—maybe it was because he still knew he had to leave me, but couldn't bring himself to do it.

Maybe I haven't let him do it, I thought suddenly. I'd been doing my very best to keep him, after all. Not that I could be faulted for that. But with everything we'd shared over the past three and a half years, including all the intimacy of the last several weeks, if Samuel still couldn't declare himself firmly on the side of sharing his future with me, then maybe he really *did* need to be with Her. I didn't want him to stay with me if that wasn't what his heart was telling him to do. And I didn't want to make things any harder or more drawn out than they needed to be, for me or for him. I still believed Samuel was a good man. I loved him and trusted him. He didn't want to hurt me. But he needed to go, apparently. And, at long last, I decided that I needed to let him.

God, take care of him, I found myself whispering, even if I was pretty sure no one was listening. *God, take care of him. Take care of us. Take care of me. I feel lost. I don't know who I am or who I should become, or what I should do. But I trust that good things will come my way again. I trust that love will come my way again. Because I have so much to give. So much I want to give. And I am giving it, now, to the man I have, to the man who has meant everything to me.*

I took my courage in both hands and wrote Samuel an email: "If you have to be with her, it's okay. You can be with her. I will let you go."

This is the climactic moment, I thought, as I left my mother's computer and went to my room to decompress. *This is that moment five pages from the end of the screenplay when the protagonist finally puts all the pieces together and realizes what they have to do. And in doing it, they complete their character arc. They grow up.*

I sat on the edge of my bed, stunned by a weighty sense of finality. There it was. The end of a long, beautiful chapter of my life. Samuel and France. Both gone. Now what?

Within twenty-four hours, I had a reply from Samuel that was only four words long: "never say that again."

It was comforting. In a way. If only I knew what it *meant*. Why did Samuel always have to be so cryptic? What other option was left for us, except for me to let Samuel go?

In the end, I could think of only one other possibility.

Just a few days later, I told Samuel in an instant message that I wanted to come to France. "I think we need to discuss this in person," I said. "Until we talk about it face to face, nothing's going to be resolved."

"How long would you come for?" he asked.

"A month?"

"What if things don't go well?"

I'd already imagined what would happen if, after a few days, it became absolutely clear that he was going to leave me for Her. I guessed I'd have to go to Paris and stay at his sister's place for a while. Or maybe I'd travel elsewhere in Europe. Go to Germany. Or Switzerland. Or Sweden. I had plenty of money saved from my time at Brandeis, even if I had been hoping to use it to buy land and build a house.

But, honestly, I didn't think I was going to have to wander around Europe. I couldn't imagine being at such odds with Samuel that we couldn't stay in the same place. No matter what the ultimate verdict on our relationship, I couldn't see us not wanting to benefit from every last moment together. "Have things ever not gone well with us?" I asked him. "I'd rather have too much time with you than too little."

"Okay," he said.

"Okay?"

"Buy your tickets."

Chapter NINE

Usually, when I set off for Europe, I was brimming with anticipation. The last time I'd flown to France, back in June, I took a moment to write in my journal, "I'm in the process of becoming someone else. Here, at Dulles Airport in Washington, sitting at the Bagel Bakery and reading *Tro Breiz*, I'm making the shift from one me to the other. I'm becoming the Frenchwoman again. The Bretonne. ... What's sure is that something is waiting for me. There's someone, and something that I don't know yet."

How true that had been! How true it had been every time I went to France.

Once, back in the first year Samuel and I were together, I'd returned to France after having been Stateside for only a couple of weeks. Arriving back in the center of Paris that September felt unusually ordinary. Mundane. The Seine just looked like a river. The Cathédrale de Notre-Dame was just a church. Hearing the French language and seeing it on newspapers and street signs had become banal. Even browsing the shelves of Gibert Joseph left me unexcited. I had already read every one of Nancy Huston's twenty books.

"But *something's* going to happen to me on this trip," I wrote in my journal, as I sat nibbling a croissant on a bench in the Jardin du Luxembourg. I opened the new novel I'd purchased at Gibert Joseph, eager to be swept away into new reflections. But I was bored before I'd even finished the first page. *Where can I find a book I want to read?* I wondered. And then, with a sudden sense of excitement, I realized the answer: *If I can't find a book I want to read, I'm going to have to write it.*

I scooped up my things and walked as fast as I could to the nearest café. I ordered a *café allongé* at the counter, and as soon as I was seated at a table, I immediately wrote in the back of my journal the first four sentences of what I knew would become a novel: "*Le hasard ? Le destin ? La providence ? C'était ces trois idées, pas d'autres, qui occupaient la pensée de Karen cet après-midi-là, après qu'elle avait raccroché le combiné et était rentrée dans la salle de bains.*" My French left a lot to be desired, but that was the language the story came out in: the story of a young American in Paris who discovers, in the space of a single afternoon, that her French boyfriend is leaving her and that she's pregnant with his child.

Until then, my approach to writing had been a very methodical, analytical one. I'd read lots of books about writing novels and screenplays, and I'd followed their advice in doing a bunch of detailed character and plot development before embarking on the first draft. But, with this novel, I paid no attention to any of that. I simply began writing the story I wanted to read. And I continued writing in order to see what my characters would do next. I put it all down in longhand, from beginning to end, in 4-by-8-inch Clairefontaine notebooks I'd purchased from Gibert Joseph's stationery store.

And I was amazed at the sudden improvement in my writing. This novel was worlds away from the stilted dialogue of my teenage screenplays and the artificial tone of the spiritual memoir I'd been struggling to get down. The improvement, I believed, came from my ability to loosen my rational grip on my writing. And that ability in turn seemed to have to do with the fact that I was writing in French.

Expressing myself in French made my grammar and idioms a bit rough, but it also freed me to follow my thoughts wherever they led. Speaking or writing in another language was almost like being in another brain. I had found throughout my year in Paris that, when I expressed myself in French, I dissociated myself much more easily from the conventions and mores attached to my native tongue. For a long while, I'd felt much more comfortable discussing sex in French than in English. '*Seins*' just sounded so much sexier than 'breasts.' And '*verge*' so much more compelling than 'dick.' I doubt I would have been capable of exploring the same subjects in my novel if I'd been writing in English. From a purely practical perspective, if it was in French, my mother couldn't read it.

All this to say that France and its language had always set me free. And, every time I'd set foot on French soil, my mind and heart had found new vistas to explore. But this time felt different. This time when I boarded the plane at Reagan National, I was nervous.

This visit with Samuel was going to be unlike any other encounter we'd ever had. I had no idea how I was going to react to seeing him under such changed circumstances. I'd felt ready to date Samuel when I'd realized how deeply I trusted him. But was that trust still intact? Now that I knew there was another woman on his mind? I didn't know if our discussions were going to be a relief or an excruciating disappointment.

As I sat waiting for the plane to take off toward my connecting flight in Philadelphia, I felt a deep loneliness creep over me. *No one can fully understand what I'm going through*, I thought. *No one can put up with me crying for as long as I need to.*

I buckled my seatbelt and stared blankly ahead as the flight attendants did their safety demonstration. Everyone else on the plane seemed so happy to be traveling, even the people who were obviously just going up to Philly on business. As we taxied out onto the runway, I leaned my head against the window. The cool glass felt good against my temple. I took several long, slow breaths as I watched the tarmac crawl by beneath us.

And then I noticed a little yellow sign planted in the grass beside the tarmac. It had only one thing printed on it: the number 33.

Right then, I wished so hard that I could believe in coincidences. Or rather, believe that they were something *more* than coincidences.

As a child, I'd read so many stories about miracles. In sixth grade, my middle-school guidance counselor had given me a copy of the autobiography of Hudson Taylor, a nineteenth-century missionary to China. I'd told her that I believed I was called to be a missionary to China, and she offered me this book as a gift of encouragement. I was wonderfully inspired by Taylor's story, especially by the fact that he refused to do as other missionaries did and ask people for money.

While Taylor was still preparing for the mission field, he had a job in London, working for an absent-minded man who asked Taylor to remind him whenever his salary was due. Taylor, however, resolved *not* to remind the man, thinking that restricting himself to prayer would be a good way to strengthen his faith. But, one week, his employer seemed entirely deaf to God's promptings, and as the week drew to a close, Taylor found himself left with only a half crown, which he needed to buy food. (He subsisted mainly on gruel.) With the half crown in his pocket, he found himself called to the bedside of a woman who had six starving children. And, as he tried to offer her spiritual comfort, he realized he couldn't do it while keeping his money for himself. So he gave all that he had to the woman and her family and returned home to eat one of his two remaining meals.

The following morning, the mail arrived just as Taylor was finishing his final bowl of gruel. Among his letters, he found an envelope from someone whose name he couldn't make out. Inside was a half sovereign: five times the amount of money he'd given away the night before.

When I was a teenager, I longed for something similarly miraculous to happen to me. And, at times, I thought it might be about to. After I'd been studying Mandarin Chinese for five years—using library books and a set of cassette tapes my parents bought me—I was beginning to wonder just how I was going to get from being a shy little homeschooler in rural Virginia to preaching to people halfway around the world. That's when a Chinese family joined my homeschool co-op. Mr. Ling, father to a couple of boisterous elementary schoolers, discovered through my mother that I was planning on being a missionary. During a rehearsal for our homeschool play, he pulled me aside in the church hallway and proceeded to tell me about his own mission trips back to China. He was so enthusiastic that he was only intermittently intelligible. "We plan another one this spring!" he exclaimed. "You come with us! You see the giant house churches the government wants to smash!"

What were the odds, I thought, that just as I was getting to the age where I could think about traveling abroad, not only did I meet a Chinese man, but one who led mission trips to China?

Granted, there was something about Mr. Ling that made me slightly uncomfortable. It had to do with the fact that he never seemed to listen to what I had to say before rushing on with his excited monologue. But, if I felt a little nervous about going into a Communist country with a man like Mr. Ling as my guide, I told myself that this was obviously what God had planned for me and not to worry because, as I'd recently read on the church bulletin board, "The safest place to be is in the center of God's will."

However, when I mentioned the prospect of the trip to my parents, they had different ideas. "We don't want you to go to China with Mr. Ling," my mother told me, in no uncertain terms.

And so I didn't. And all my other supposed acts of providence fizzled out in similar fashion. When I had to decide where to go to college, for instance, I prayed for God's guidance. "If you want me to go to Messiah College," I said to him one morning as I was getting out of the shower, "let my acceptance letter come today." To my astonishment, it did. But then, when I got to Messiah, it seemed like the college experience drew me *away* from God, not toward him. My conversations with Daniel, my classes on critical thinking, and my Bible course on the Pentateuch combined in such a way that, for the first time ever, I was able to picture the world without God. And once the possibility of God's non-existence entered my mind, I realized that I didn't have any evidence to prove it wasn't the truth. Which led me to that night in Nancy when I tearfully prayed, "Please, God, if you're there, just give me some kind of sign."

That sign had never come. And it felt much too late to start looking for it now.

As the plane continued to inch down the tarmac, the bleak landscape of the runways and the gray sky above did nothing to make the universe seem any less lonely. Here we were, just a bunch of people sitting on a plane, doing the best we could to avoid the worst the world had to offer but sometimes getting dragged through some pretty deep shit—each of us ultimately all alone.

Then, a few yards farther down the tarmac, we passed another sign. It was small and yellow like the first one. And once again it had nothing on it but the number 33.

I had to smile in spite of myself. I knew that, if Samuel were there, he'd be pointing it out to me and probably scribbling some notes about it on the edge of his boarding pass, later to be typed into the journal he kept on his laptop. I thought about writing a note myself. But I was pretty sure I would remember this without any help.

Just a few seconds later, we passed yet another sign reading "33." And then we passed another. And another. My smile got wider. *So you don't believe in signs, huh? Even yellow ones that are two feet square?*

As I looked more closely, I saw that, between the yellow signs, there were also white numerals painted on the asphalt of the connecting taxiways. They, too, said "33." And suddenly, from somewhere deep within me, came the distinct feeling that something—or Someone—was clearly telling me, "You are *not* alone."

I understood, of course, that 33 was the number of the runway. It wasn't like these were just random signs that all happened to bear the same number. But even my deep-seated skepticism of the idea of synchronicities couldn't prevent me from feeling that this runway number—and the sheer quantity of signs displaying it—was designed to get my attention. I didn't have the energy to analyze the feeling or calculate the probabilities involved. All I knew was that, as the plane accelerated down the runway, I was able to shut my eyes and relax for the first time in a long while.

Unfortunately, by the time we landed in Philadelphia and I boarded my second flight—this one to Paris—the feeling of calm had worn off. In the new plane, I had a seat in the middle section, far from any windows, so I had no way of knowing if we were again on Runway 33. I felt the sadness creeping back over me, tightening my jaw and causing little shudders in my chest as I tried to prevent the escape of a sob. I couldn't avoid thinking about what awaited me in France. Would Samuel be happy to see me? Would our month together be a joyful reunion or an unbearable tearing apart of everything we'd shared?

When I got to Paris, I was going to take a train to Brittany to meet Samuel. I already had the ticket in my carry-on, and I pulled it out to check how much time I'd have to transfer. I hated having to run through passport control and baggage claim. But what I noticed when I glanced at the ticket was not the departure time. It was my seat assignment: Seat 33.

Suddenly I was crying—and not just a few tears. A river. They just poured down my face into my lap. I knew people all around me were staring, but it made no difference. However much my head wanted to say that this 33 was just a coincidence, my heart had a different idea. My heart felt that there was someone who knew exactly what I'd been feeling these last few weeks, someone who knew exactly how deep the hurt and despair ran. I felt that that Someone wanted me to *know* that they knew. They wanted me to know that, as I rode that train to meet Samuel, they would be with me. In Seat 33.

When I stepped off the train in Vannes, there he was: the man I hadn't known if I would ever see again, standing on the platform in a dark blue sweater and gray corduroy jacket and looking a little worse for wear. Had he lost weight? He had a few days' worth of stubble and a solemn—maybe nervous—expression.

"*Salut*," I said as I approached, dragging a rolling suitcase with each hand. I thought about having told him "*adieu*" just a few weeks ago. "*Au revoir*" would have been more appropriate after all.

"*Salut*," he replied.

We didn't hug or kiss. Just took each other in.

"Let me get your bags," Samuel said finally, and I let him take them. The smaller one was packed solid with books he had left in the States and that I figured he would want to have if we did definitively break up. "Do you want something to eat?" he asked. "Or drink?"

Over email, we'd discussed whether I should take the train to where Samuel was currently living with his dad, or to Vannes, which was closer to the family beach house where we were going to stay during my visit. We'd decided I should arrive directly in Vannes, so we wouldn't have to start our visit with a long car ride. I felt the wisdom of that now. I wanted to be able to sit with Samuel face to face. "Let's get some coffee," I said.

We sat down across from each other at a little metal table in the café area of the train station, and Samuel handed me the laminated menu. I stared at it for a moment, then realized I didn't want anything. "Do *you* want anything?" I asked.

"I already had something, while I was waiting for you," he said. He gestured to the table pushed up next to ours, where a plastic tray with an empty paper espresso cup sat. "We don't have to order anything."

I put the menu aside and just looked at him, searching his face for some clue as to why he had done all this to me. And whether he regretted it enough to change his mind. He looked intently back at me. Maybe he was searching for his own answers?

I wanted to take his hands in mine, but I didn't know if he wanted me to. Was he waiting for me to make a move, or did he think I should be waiting for him? Who had chosen the distance between us? Had *he* chosen it, in saying that he couldn't marry me and that he might be in love with another woman? Or had *I* chosen it, in refusing to be patient while he wrestled with his uncertainties?

Finally, I extended a hand, and he immediately clasped it in both of his. His palms were warm. Comforting. "Sharon, I'm so sorry."

"I know," I said.

I sighed and glanced outside. "It's a pretty cloudy day, isn't it?"

"Breton weather," said Samuel.

I smiled a tired smile, knowing how much he liked clouds and rain. "Maybe we should go," I said.

We made our way out to the car. Samuel squeezed my bags into the trunk of his Renault while I watched. Then he closed the hatchback and took a tentative step toward me. I stepped toward him as well, and he wrapped his arms around me and held me tight. I pressed my nose into his shoulder, drinking in the familiar smell of his corduroy jacket.

I thought of all the corrosive moments of loneliness I'd experienced over the last month and a half. The long nights spent lying awake in bed, longing for the touch of Samuel's lips, and the rainy days in North Carolina when I wished we could do so much more than email each other. As I thought of each moment I'd spent longing for him, I clung to him more tightly. Samuel, too, seemed incapable of getting me close enough. When we finally let go, we just looked at each other's tear-stained faces without saying a word.

We dropped my bags off at the beach house, a cozy little space with a living/dining room downstairs and two bedrooms upstairs, everything decorated in a blue and white nautical theme. The south-facing sliding glass doors looked out onto a windswept lawn dotted with scrubby coastal trees and mounds of bay laurel and lavender. If you stood at exactly the right spot on the balcony, you could look through a break in the next row of apartments and see a bluish gray line of ocean.

We went out to dinner that night, to a *crêperie*, where I got my usual *chèvre-miel*. We talked about mundane things: the new book Samuel was writing, his sister's job in Paris. It was nice to know that we had not just hours to talk, but days and weeks. I knew that our finding each other again was probably not a permanent thing. We were very likely going to have to say goodbye again, and in a more definitive way this time. But, for those first twenty-four hours, I wouldn't let myself think of anything but the fact that we were together now. In the days before I left the States, my sister Sarah (who was also living at home at the time) had been listening to a song from the *Twilight: Eclipse* soundtrack. Natasha Khan's haunting voice now played over and over in my head: "*Let's Get Lost.*" Even if it was only for a single night, I desperately needed to lose myself in this present moment, this moment in which Samuel and I were reunited.

I had told Samuel before booking my tickets that I expected to sleep in the same bed with him while I was in France. "If that's not okay, then I can't come," I'd told him. So when we came back to the house after dinner and started brushing our teeth and getting ready for bed, *that* question, at least, had already been settled.

We climbed the polished wood stairs to the master bedroom. It was chilly, and Samuel turned on the space heater. We each went to our own side of the double bed, and I turned away from him slightly as I slipped out of my clothes and into my pajamas. I heard his jeans fall to the floor. When I turned back around, he was under the duvet, lying on his back, eyes closed. I slid between the sheets.

"Can I turn the light off?" asked Samuel.

"*Ouais.*"

He flicked off the lamp sitting on the little wooden table by his head.

In the darkness, I pulled myself up against Samuel's warm body. He put his arm gently around me. We lay there silently awhile, feeling our old closeness. Then, as the moments passed, a familiar feeling of suspense arose: *Are we going to make love, or aren't we?*

Samuel moved slightly, and I felt his breath on my face. I tilted my chin up just enough for my lips to meet his. This was the kiss I had dreamed of every night alone in my bed in Virginia, when my chest had felt under such pressure from yearning and disappointment that I'd wondered if I would survive to see the morning. Now this kiss seemed capable of healing all its ill effects. My worn, lonely body—

pushed to the breaking point in its longing for the one it loved—now relaxed into his arms, soaking up his return in all its warmth and tenderness.

"Do you want to make love?" asked Samuel.

"Yes," I said, with absolute conviction.

Afterward, I just held Samuel to me and sobbed.

That first week together was very hard, but there were some moments of calm, like when Samuel was sitting at the dining table typing the book he was currently working on and I was curled up on the couch reading Judith Thurman's biography of Isak Dinesen. Isak Dinesen was the pen name of Karen Blixen, the real-life heroine of *Out of Africa*, and Thurman quoted her as saying, "To love [God] truly you must love change, and you must love a joke, these being the true inclinations of his own heart." I read the quote to Samuel, and we managed a chuckle or two at the huge joke God was currently playing on us. But much of that first week we spent in tears and anger.

A couple of days in, Samuel and I had our first real talk. We were sitting at the table, having just finished a breakfast of toasted baguette with butter and raspberry jam, along with two cups of Samuel's very strong coffee. He would get up in the morning while it was still dark, and the first thing he would do, even before going to the bathroom or getting dressed, was fill his Italian coffee pot with grounds and set it to heat on the stove.

"I need you to tell me what's going on," I said, and took a sip. "I need you to *explain*."

He sighed a sigh of overwhelming fatigue. "I don't think I can, Sharon. I can't even explain it to myself."

I inwardly rolled my eyes. "Well, then just tell me this. Are you going to leave me for her?"

"Sharon, I...." He rubbed his forehead as though trying to massage his brain into action. "I don't think I have a choice."

"What do you mean, you don't have a *choice*?"

"I think this is what I have to do. I'm sorry."

I asked him more questions, digging and prodding in an effort to get a more coherent response out of him. But no matter how many questions I posed, or how gently and understandingly I asked them, I couldn't get an answer that made any more sense than that.

Ultimately, there was only one way I could understand his behavior: he had to be in love with this other woman. That was the only thing he wouldn't be able to explain to me. I didn't want it to be true. And it was hard to believe that it *was* true, seeing how little time they had spent together compared to the time Samuel had spent with me. But it seemed obvious, now that I was actually able to admit the thought to consciousness. All this talk about God's will, and how he didn't want to do this but he had to, was really just cover for the plain and simple fact that he loved this other woman and wanted to be with her more than he wanted to be with me. Despite his negative response to my attempt to let him go—"never say that again"—I suspected more and more that this grand gift I had been attempting to give him—this enormously patient, unconditional love—was something ultimately unnecessary, and possibly undesired. All his protests to the contrary.

That night in bed, as both Samuel and I lay there unable to fall asleep, I wondered if he was thinking of her. "Do you wish you were with her right now instead of me?" I asked.

"No," he replied. "I most certainly do not."

He rolled toward me and took me in his arms. "I don't have any desire to rush that day. I'm not ready to say goodbye to you. I *love* you, Sharon."

But if he loved me, how could he even conceive of leaving me? And if he loved *her*, why didn't he want to be with her as soon as possible? What the hell was going on?

One morning, Samuel suggested that we shake up our usual routine and go out for breakfast. He made reservations at a hotel restaurant right on the water, and at 7:30, before the sun had even come up, we walked down the beach in a misty rain to our rendezvous.

The restaurant turned out to be empty except for us. It was the off season, and the wet weather had probably discouraged any customers who might have otherwise shown up. We had our pick of tables and chose one beside a huge window looking out over the ocean. We could see a few hardy souls out on the rocky beach in waders, harvesting mollusks. Samuel and I ordered omelets and croissants, with coffee and orange juice. "*Je t'invite*," said Samuel. My treat.

He found a copy of the day's paper on the counter of the bar and read me the headlines, with his usual commentary about coincidences. I nodded and smiled and looked out at the waves washing up on the shore. It was such a cozy feeling, being snugly inside while it was cold and drizzly beyond the window.

"This is a perfect morning, isn't it?" said Samuel.

"*Oui. Absolument.*"

For the space of that one morning, I could believe that everything was going to be all right.

The next afternoon, we were back to our usual routine. Samuel was at the dining table on his laptop, preparing some remarks for the book fair we were going to be attending in western Brittany the next day. I was on the couch with *Isak Dinesen: The Life of a Storyteller*. I was reading about Karen Blixen's relationship with Thorkild Bjørnvig and came across this sentence: "But when she returned to Denmark he went to Brittany, to a hotel by the sea." I chuckled and read it aloud to Samuel.

He smiled. "The more attentive you are to coincidences, the more there are."

I stared out the window for a moment, then turned back to Samuel. "I just want you to know how much I love you," I said. "You don't have to say it back. I just want you to know."

Samuel nodded.

A few minutes later, he looked up at me again. "I wish it could be otherwise, Sharon. But I think I'm going to have to be with her."

For crying out loud, why do you have to say that now? For once, I just wanted to scream. I just wanted Samuel to understand the hell he was putting me through. Instead, I swallowed and glared at the floor, my eyebrows knit together in a fierce expression that, if Samuel had been looking at me, would have made clear to him my state of mind. But he'd gone back to his computer.

I managed to hold myself together until we went to bed that night. We were both tired, and we didn't make love. We lay on our backs, not touching, just breathing heavily into the pitch dark of the tiny bedroom. Then I started to cry. There were only a few tears at first, gathering in the corners of my eyes. But then they started falling, and my chest started heaving. Before I knew it, I had turned over onto my stomach and was sobbing rivers into my pillow.

I knew my crying wasn't going to do any good. I knew my pain wasn't going to make Samuel change his mind. If anything, it would make him more distant. But I couldn't help it. The disappointment, the sadness, the longing were simply too great. They had to come out.

I felt Samuel there, aware of what was going on. But he didn't touch me. And he didn't say a word. Maybe he knew there was only one thing that would truly comfort me. And that he couldn't say it.

But it was too much for me to be lost in such grief and feel Samuel refraining from holding me. I shoved the covers back, rolled out of bed, and went downstairs. I didn't bother to put any clothes on, even though the house was cold, with its tile floor and cinderblock walls. I lay down on the living room rug and curled up in a ball. There was a blanket on the couch, but I didn't pull it over me. I needed my naked, chilly body. I needed to act out my desperation—my agony.

After I'd lain there for ten minutes, sobbing and shivering, Samuel came down to check on me. He bent over my head. "Shahone, please. I hate to see you like this. Come back to bed."

"Just leave me alone."

"Shahone." He pulled the blanket off the couch and tucked it around me. "Shahone, I'm so sorry."

I heard him go to the bathroom. A few minutes later he slowly climbed the stairs back to the bedroom. But I stayed on the floor. This was the end. All the love I'd given Samuel—and was still giving him—hadn't made a dent. Love, it turned out, was just not enough.

When I finally felt exhausted enough to sleep, I put the blanket back on the couch and crept up the wooden stairs to the bedroom. I slid under the covers without touching Samuel. Thankfully, within a few minutes, I was out.

Samuel and I were supposed to leave the next morning to go to the book fair. We'd planned to spend two nights in a hotel and had both been looking forward to it. But, when the gray light of morning filtered into the house, I was still so angry that I couldn't face the idea of traveling with Samuel, and certainly not of sitting for two days straight in a book stall making small talk with French strangers.

Samuel was packing his duffel bag, and I just sat sullenly on the couch. "Are you ready?" he asked, when he saw me stiff as a statue.

"I'm going to let you go by yourself," I said.

"What?" He seemed genuinely surprised. Did he really think I'd be able to soldier on indefinitely in this heartbreaking state?

"I can't face it right now," I told him.

"You're going to stay here alone? Without a car?"

"I need the time to myself. I can walk to the grocery store. And the *boulangerie*. Would you just take me to the bookstore before you go? So I can buy something to read?"

The nearest bookstore we knew of was the FNAC, a twenty-minute drive into Vannes. I sat silently in the passenger seat of the Renault as Samuel wove through all the roundabouts. Partly I was being stubborn, but mostly I was just exhausted. And what was there left to say anyway?

When we got to the FNAC, I went wordlessly through the automatic doors and straight to the fiction section. This was an area I rarely visited, except for the year I'd spent reading Nancy Huston. I usually preferred nonfiction. Books about "real" life. Sociology, ecology, physics. But today I needed some escape from reality. So I looked through the novels and found Irène Némirovsky's *Les Chiens et les Loups* and Muriel Barbery's *L'élégance du hérisson*. I also bought one book of nonfiction: the memoir of a Swiss woman who left behind her boyfriend and her very lucrative career to live in a hut in Kenya with a Maasai man she'd met on vacation.

Samuel drove me back to the house and gave me his cell phone. "I'll call you from a pay phone tonight at seven," he said. "Please pick up. So I know you're okay."

I nodded and set the phone on the dining table where I'd hear it.

When the door clicked shut behind Samuel, my eyes got watery, but I dabbed them dry with a square of toilet tissue torn from the roll I'd taken to carrying around the house with me.

In one corner of the living area, there was a blue collapsible camping chair that was wonderfully comfortable—it hugged you like a hammock. I pulled it over to the window. The sun had burned off the clouds by then, and I settled myself under its rays, with my three new books and a mug of mint tea.

I realized I had been right about needing the solitude. I could feel my entire being relaxing into the emptiness of the house. I needed this time and space alone to generate some new energy—to remember that I *had* an energy source that didn't depend on Samuel. I read all that morning and into the afternoon.

Around four o'clock, I walked into the village to the *boulangerie* and bought a baguette and a *pain au chocolat*. Something about walking around in Samuel's town without Samuel made the tears surface again. I walked quickly back past all the white-washed, blue-shuttered vacation cottages with their carefully tended rose gardens and shut myself safely in the house again. I ate my *pain au chocolat* and went back to reading about how surprised the Swiss woman was when she learned that her Maasai husband wouldn't ever kiss her, not even while they were making love.

Samuel called at seven, just like he'd said he would. I was finishing my dinner of pasta and buttered baguette. "*Comment tu vas?*" he asked.

"Fine. I think it's good for me to have some time alone."

We were both quiet.

"Where are you staying?" I asked.

"At a hostel."

"Why don't you go to a hotel?"

"There's no point in spending the money if you're not with me."

"Mm."

"I miss you, Shahone."

"I miss you, too."

I slept well that night, alone in the bed. And I woke up early the next morning. I made more tea and went right back to my blue chair.

As I read, I felt some of my faith in life returning. *Whatever happens, you will survive*, I told myself, and felt it to be true. The goodness of my life did not depend on Samuel. I would find many good things even once we were forced to separate.

A funny thing happened, though, as I became more comfortable with the idea of Samuel and me going our separate ways. The better I was able to accept that we were going to have to part, the more I realized I wanted to enjoy every remaining moment we had together. We still had two and a half weeks left, after all. I felt myself wanting to make the most of it. If only Samuel would come back early from his weekend away…I wouldn't shut him out anymore.

He called again that evening. "How was the fair?" I asked.

"All right. Tons of coincidences. But I didn't sell any books. I'm thinking of not staying for the second day, coming back tonight. Would that be okay?"

"Yes," I said. "I would love to see you."

I waited up for him, putting some quiet music on the stereo. I read by the light of the little blue lamp I'd brought downstairs from the bedroom. Finally, around 10:30, I heard Samuel's key in the lock. I stayed sitting on the couch until he'd gotten in the door and seen me there. Then I went to him. "Hey," I said, and kissed him on the mouth. "It's really nice to have you back."

He dumped his duffel bag on the floor and pulled me gently into his arms. "Let's go to bed."

Chapter TEN

One evening, Samuel and I were sitting around reading after dinner, and I was thinking over the string of 33s I'd experienced in the last few weeks, culminating with the signs on the tarmac and my seat number on the train. They'd gotten me seriously considering for the first time in four years that God might actually exist. But I was still wary of interpreting the facts in this way, for reasons I've already explained. After all, what were the odds that a God who had never spoken to me before was going to start now, when I was twenty-nine years old? And if he had ignored all those desperate pleas of mine in the past, was he a God I wanted to have around anyway?

There was a real difference, though, between my reaction to these 33s and my reaction to those other "signs" when I was a child and teenager: I didn't assume I knew what they meant. I didn't assume that they proved the existence of the very specific God I'd learned about in Sunday School, the conservative Judeo-Christian God who was disappointed every time I stopped reading the Bible or didn't evangelize someone I passed on the street. The God who sent those who didn't believe in him to hell. I knew that these signs could instead be communications from a very different kind of God—or from no God at all. What was clear was that, when I encountered the 33s on the plane, I felt a *presence*. I felt that they were telling me, very simply, "You are not alone."

"What are you thinking about?" Samuel asked, when he saw that I'd abandoned the book I was reading to stare off into space.

"Oh…coincidences."

He smiled. "Remember Hulkamania?"

Actually, I'd forgotten until he brought it up. The story of Hulkamania started my senior year of college, when my roommates and I found a giant Hulk Hogan beer stein abandoned in a dorm kitchen and—for some reason lost to the ages—adopted it as our mascot. Every year after graduation, we got together for a roommate reunion, and every year we made sure the Hulkamania stein was present. Until one year when the stein had a nasty encounter with a concrete floor. After that, we were forced to endure one steinless roommate reunion. But, thankfully, the following year my friend Debbie came to the rescue, with an exact replica she'd located on eBay.

Samuel had attended the reunion where we inaugurated the new Hulkamania stein. We held a ceremony, in which Debbie solemnly read from the back of stein the blurb describing Hulk Hogan's strength and valor. And then we all climbed into our cars to go on a picnic.

The picnic site was a few miles away, hidden along one of the winding back roads of southeastern Pennsylvania. As our caravan of vehicles rounded a bend, we were astonished to find ourselves driving past an extraordinarily timely piece of lawn art. To our great surprise, some local Hulk Hogan fan had covered the slope in their front yard with yellow and orange gravel, which they had meticulously arranged to spell "Hulkamania"—in the exact colors as on our newly inaugurated stein. I have never seen anything else related to Hulk Hogan on anyone else's lawn, before or since that day.

Samuel had been as stunned by the coincidence as any of the rest of us. Now, looking back, he told me how he had understood its meaning. "God was telling you that what you were doing was very good."

"You mean getting together every year?"

"*Oui*," he confirmed. "Your friendship."

What now surprised me most was that I hadn't spent more time marveling at this coincidence in the months since it occurred. "I'm not sure I believe in God," I told Samuel. "But *if* I believe, it's because of that."

The next day was a particularly gray one, even for Brittany. There was a brief moment of sunshine in the morning, when Samuel and I took a walk on the stony beach and I stripped off my shoes and socks so I could feel the smooth, algae-covered rocks against the soles of my feet and dip my toes into the icy rivulets that ran between them. But then the clouds returned, rain began to fall, and we retreated to the house and our usual business of reading and writing.

After lunch, a slight melancholy hung over the room. Usually, I was the first to want to get up and do something, but this time it was Samuel. "Let's go to that new *librairie*," he suggested. Recently, while riding our bikes, we'd seen signs for a used-book store one town over.

"It's raining," I protested.

"It's okay. We'll drive. Come on." He took my arm and pulled me from my spot on the couch.

As we turned onto the main road that linked the two towns, it was still raining slightly, but through the mist we could see a rainbow.

The end of it was planted directly in the middle of the town where we were headed, as if the bookstore were our pot of gold.

"Do you know what rainbows mean in the Bible?" I asked Samuel. "After Noah's flood, God put a rainbow in the sky as a sign of his covenant with humankind never to bring that kind of disaster on them again." I silently wondered if this Breton rainbow was God promising never again to bring this kind of disaster on *me*—the loss of the man and the life I held so dear.

The bookshop was in a small stone house wedged between a bar and a *crêperie*, both of which were closed for the winter. While the empty neighboring businesses looked cold and sad, the light pouring from the bookshop windows was radiating warmth and welcome, and I knew we'd been right to come. Inside, a middle-aged woman wrapped in several colorful scarves stood behind the register, chatting with a couple who had just made a purchase. Samuel and I slid quietly past them, into a space filled with the twinkle of Christmas lights, the scent of old paper, and the sounds of classic American jazz.

A book jumped out at me from the very first shelf I passed: *La chamane blanche*. The White Shaman. For most of my life I'd shied away from learning much about indigenous cultures. Their animistic spirituality was taboo in evangelical Christian circles—my mother never even allowed my sisters and me to have dream catchers in our bedrooms—and it had never occurred to me to revise this attitude until sometime in graduate school, when I met an intriguing woman at a Christian philosophy conference. She was one of the keynote speakers and did research in both artificial intelligence and theology. I was very impressed with her work, and delighted when we ended up riding back to the airport in the same vehicle. During the ride, she ended up telling me about a trip she'd taken to Australia and her surprising experiences with telepathy there. She said she met an aboriginal woman who knew details of her daughter's life hundreds of miles away in the city without ever talking to her on the phone. She added that there was scientific research to back this up.

It was not the sort of thing I had ever expected to hear from a Christian. Or from a researcher in artificial intelligence, for that matter. But this professor had established her credibility with me over the course of the conference, and I was intrigued enough to want to investigate.

That's how I found myself, a few years later, reading a copy of *Black Elk Speaks*, a record of the visions of a North American shaman. That book was completely different from anything I'd come across before. Fascinating. But at the same time, reading about Black Elk's uncanny supernatural experiences as I sat alone in my apartment in Massachusetts seriously creeped me out. I had to put the book away before I got even halfway through. I just had too much fear surrounding the idea of spiritual entities that could appear at any time, in any place, and were not primarily comforting figures.

Such was my meager background in the subject matter when I came across *The White Shaman* that day in the bookstore. Interestingly, I realized as soon as I saw it that I had seen the very same book the previous week at the FNAC. This made me think it was probably a fairly new release, but when I checked the copyright date, I saw that it had been published over ten years ago. Seeing an old book like that twice in two weeks seemed rather like a sign, so I put it under my arm.

As I continued to browse the shelves, I came upon a book by Claude Michelet. I had just recently discovered Michelet, who was basically the French counterpart of Wendell Berry. I'd started one of his novels about rural life in the Limousin in the early twentieth century, and now I found a book where he told his own life story, about rejecting the professional life his parents had envisioned for him and becoming a farmer instead. *J'ai choisi la terre*, it was called. I chose the land. It seemed like another obvious pick.

In the middle of the bookstore, amid the labyrinth of shelves, sat a woodstove with two small settees positioned to face it. I took a seat and began perusing those two books, as well as another one I found on the shelf beside the settee: *Les chemins de la sagesse*, The Ways of Wisdom, by a Hindu Christian named Arnaud Desjardins. Samuel had been accumulating a stack of his own, and he settled it beside him on the other couch. We sat there together, reading our finds while the flames danced behind the glass door of the woodstove and Miles Davis improvised quietly in the background. I felt a deep sense of rest. Suddenly, everything surrounding Samuel and me was warm and comfortable, with all of our problems and worries having momentarily dissolved into the cozy atmosphere of the shop.

At the same time, I felt a quiver of excitement. These three books, it seemed to me, were *exactly* the ones I needed at that moment. Each of them promised to answer some important question I'd been pondering. For instance: *Are there realms of reality that transcend the Western, scientific worldview? Am I crazy to be leaving academic life for manual labor on a farm? What's the purpose of all this emotional pain I'm going through?*

As closing time approached, Samuel and I pulled ourselves from the embrace of the couches and made our way to the register. The owner chatted with us amiably as she totaled our order on her little pad. "Come back soon!" she urged, handing us our purchases. She took one of her business cards from the holder in front of the register and gave it to Samuel. "Next time you come, I'll make you *chocolat chaud!*"

When we emerged from the shop, we found that the rain had finally ceased and the sky had cleared. The setting sun was bathing all the buildings on the block in a slanting yellow light. "This was a perfect afternoon," I told Samuel, squeezing his hand as we walked toward the courtyard gate to the street. "A gift from God." I gave him a peck on the cheek.

"Did you notice the address?" he asked, inclining his head back toward the shop.

I froze. I hadn't noticed, but I had a pretty good idea of what I would see when I turned around. "*T'es sérieux?*" I said. I turned back toward the shop, and my eyes came to rest on the little blue plaque next to the door: 33.

Samuel handed me the owner's card: "33, Grande Rue," it read. I buried my face in his shoulder and wept.

In the midst of the most difficult month of our lives, when Samuel and I were day after day struggling valiantly to do right by each other despite how tired and wounded we were, it seemed God had decided to give us this little bookstore as a resting place: a cozy way station in which to recharge our spirits. It couldn't have been a more perfectly timed moment of grace. And just so there could be no mistake about where this gift had come from, God had left us God's initials.

Samuel drove us home by a road that ran along the beach. The dunes were too high for us to see the sea from the street, but about halfway back to the house, we came up on a slight rise where I caught a glimpse of the magnificent sunset taking place over the water. "*Arrête la voiture!*" I shouted. As soon as Samuel stopped the car, I jumped out and ran toward the wooden steps that led to the ocean, Samuel hard on my heels.

Just as we came up over the top of the dunes, the sun broke into the cleft between two towering cumulonimbus clouds, and a beam of brilliant orange light shot across the water and up the sand to meet our faces. "Here I am," I felt it saying, in a language more powerful than words. "You thought you were alone, but Here I Am."

I basked, speechless, in the glow of this arresting display. After a moment, I noticed a flock of small seabirds flying low over the waves. Every few seconds, they banked and changed course, all at the very same moment. There was something so beautiful and effortless about their movement, something that testified to a deep harmony underlying all things. And suddenly I couldn't escape the feeling that God's reason for almost taking Samuel away from me was to bring me to this moment. For me to see God—here, on this day—and for me to know that it was God who had given me Samuel in the first place.

Until that moment, I would never have believed myself capable of saying that suffering—true, prolonged suffering—could be an essential spiritual tool. In my college days, I had wrestled with the perennial problem of how a good God could allow the intense and widespread suffering that exists in the world. I hadn't been able to imagine any spiritual goal great enough to outweigh that suffering and at the same time make it necessary. But, in that moment at the top of the dunes when I saw the sky break open and the light come pouring through, I suddenly found myself thinking that this bit of theology I'd always hated might actually make sense.

"If you have never truly suffered," I wrote in my journal later, "if you have never lost the thing you thought was essential to your happiness, even to your life itself, then you will always fear this experience. But if you go through it, perhaps then you will be liberated from it." I realized that a broken heart—like the cleft in a cloud—allowed the light to shine through. And the only goal that could have been worth so much suffering was precisely this: to feel the very presence of God.

That evening, I recorded all the events of the day in my journal, beginning with our morning walk on the beach. My journal at the time was a notebook I'd been given by Messiah College as a graduation gift. It was titled "Stepping stones: Getting your feet wet," and on the cover was a drawing of a woman's bare feet stepping from one black rock to another. It was a picture of exactly what I'd been doing that morning on the beach. Seeing that, I had the deep conviction that all of this had been planned. Orchestrated. And beautifully performed down to the smallest detail.

After writing my notes about the events of the day, I dove back into the books I'd bought. By now, I had a strong suspicion that whoever or whatever was out there in the universe had intentionally put these books on my path, and I was anxious to find out why. I started with *La chamane blanche*.

In this book, Russian psychiatrist Olga Kharitidi described her first encounters with the shamanism of Siberia. A friend of hers who was desperately ill persuaded her to come along on a trip to seek healing from a shaman in a remote mountain village. This shaman, a woman, proceeded to put Kharitidi's friend through an excruciatingly painful ceremony, at the end of which she was decisively healed. This floored Kharitidi, who had a thoroughly Western, scientific sensibility. But perhaps even more unexpected than the healing was the shaman's announcement to Kharitidi that Kharitidi was meant to become her apprentice. The psychiatrist, not surprisingly, rejected this idea out of hand. But when she returned home to the city, she began experiencing strange visions, to the point that she finally consented to return to the village and learn the art. That is how she became a "white" shaman, and acquired some amazingly effective techniques for healing patients she had previously considered beyond hope.

Reading her book, I was curious to know whether I would find similarities between the "supernatural" experiences Kharitidi described and those I'd come across in my brief readings on Native American and Australian aboriginal cultures. Major similarities, I thought, would be evidence that the experiences reported were real. But what struck me most in *La chamane blanche* was the uniqueness of the spiritual beings that appeared to Siberian shamans. For instance, Kharitidi was frequently appeared to by a woman in a fur coat riding on a white horse, who corresponded to a character from Siberian mythology.

Because this wasn't what I'd been expecting, I was tempted to doubt the truth of the reports. But, instead, I tried putting my skepticism on the back burner and asking myself, "What if all these accounts—the ones in this book as well as those from other cultures—*were* true?" As I reflected on this possibility, I felt a new, compelling idea crystallize. If all these stories were true, it would mean that the "spiritual" world did not manifest itself in a single, uniform fashion, but instead manifested itself to each culture or individual according to that culture or individual's mode of understanding. It would imply that the spiritual world manifested itself *using the symbolic language of its audience.*

Suddenly the idea from quantum mechanics that what someone observes depends to some extent on what they *expect* to observe took on newly colorful implications. Could it be that, if proponents of the naturalistic, scientific worldview didn't encounter the "supernatural," it was because they weren't looking for it? Could it be that each of us got more or less the world we imagined to exist—the proponents of a mechanistic, physicalist worldview being no exception? Maybe if you believed only in objective, collectively verifiable phenomena, that's all you would find. But if you believed that reality could speak differently to different observers, maybe you'd find *that.*

On the other hand, I'd believed for many years in a personal Judeo-Christian God, and I'd found pitiful little evidence of his existence.

When I finished *La chamane blanche*, I turned to the book by the Hindu Christian Arnaud Desjardins. I'd already read one of his works, a book called *Spiritualité: De quoi s'agit-il?* Spirituality: What's It About? Samuel had given that book to me for my last birthday, because its title echoed the question he'd asked me on our first date. He reassured me

I didn't have to read it—it was just a symbolic gift, he said—but I found myself curious. And, when I started reading it over the summer, I discovered that Desjardins' take on spirituality was completely different from what I'd expected. Indeed, it was different from any view I'd previously encountered.

The purpose of spirituality, Desjardins explained, was to *liberate*: to liberate people from whatever is constraining or limiting them, including the strictures of religious doctrine. He explained that true spirituality is about being free from anxiety, fear, and worry. Which sounded strangely like some things Jesus had said. "Do not worry about tomorrow, for tomorrow will worry about itself," and, "Who of you by worrying can add a single hour to his life?" Furthermore, Jesus had nothing but contempt for the organized religion of his day—he called the religious leaders snakes and white-washed tombs—and nothing but grace and mercy for those who had been condemned for not adhering to the rules laid out by the religious "authorities."

What would it mean, I wondered, to free ourselves from the shackles of *today's* religious dogmas? Could it really be that, if there was a God, God didn't care whether I read my Bible? Or how often I prayed? Or whether I evangelized? I remembered how, some months after I'd declared myself an atheist in college, I'd had a moment when I'd started to wonder whether there might be a God after all. I was immediately overcome by dread: dread of having to go back to reading my Bible every morning. But then I felt a little voice in my head say, "Just take a break from reading your Bible, okay?" The idea that *that* voice—that comforting, liberating voice—could be God's...that was revolutionary to me. In exactly the way Desjardins described.

Now I picked up this other book I'd found by Desjardins. *Les chemins de la sagesse*, it was called. The Paths of Wisdom. And its recurring refrain was that, in order to find liberation, we need to accept suffering. In fact, Desjardins was saying that liberation comes from accepting *all* the things we don't like, because at the deepest level of reality there is no distinction between good and bad. From our limited perspective, some things *appear* to us as things to be sought and others as things to be avoided, but in reality, it often turns out that the things we most strenuously avoid do us the most good.

After my recent experience, I could actually see what he was saying. Good, as he said, was not situated *opposite* bad. Rather, good was *beyond* bad. Good was what resulted when we traversed the seemingly worst experiences of our lives and came out unafraid on the other side.

Desjardins insisted that one of the most important things to learn was how to permit ourselves to feel our suffering fully, and so allow it to move through us quickly and unimpeded. I knew that when I felt myself besieged by negative emotions—when, for instance, the thought of never seeing Samuel again clamped down on my heart like a vice—my first instinct was to push the feeling away, to force myself to think happy thoughts instead. But, after reading Desjardins, I decided to try his approach instead.

The next time I felt the approach of that familiar mixture of sadness, grief, and despair, I lowered my book into my lap, closed my eyes, and just let it come. I imagined myself lying on a comfortable bed, letting the feelings simply flow over me. This didn't stop them from coming—or from hurting—but in my lack of resistance, I did feel a measure of relief. I felt unthreatened, more like a passive observer than a true sufferer. And as I sat there observing my feelings, I started to ask myself some new questions. *Why does the thought of losing Samuel paralyze me with fear?* I wondered. *Is there some deeper worry being touched here? Am I maybe afraid that I won't merely be without Samuel's company, but without anyone's at all? Am I afraid that I'm all alone in the universe?*

As soon as I'd phrased the question that way, I knew the answer: *Yes. Yes, I am.*

Over the next minute or so, the fear and grief rapidly diminished. It was as though I had watched them arrive and flow over me, and now I was watching them move off in the other direction, receding toward the horizon. And there I was, still sitting on the sofa. Intact.

I began using this technique frequently, and it worked quite reliably. At least during the day. The dead of night was a different story. The pain always seemed much stronger then, and my ability to sit by and calmly observe it vaporized. *That book is a bunch of bullshit!* I yelled inside my head one night around 2am, when I awoke with the realization that, in only a week, I would have to say goodbye to Samuel for good. I writhed under the covers, trying to quietly feel and release the hurt, but the pain in my chest was just too much for me to deal with in silence. Especially when Samuel was sleeping there beside me, making me furious in his complete obliviousness.

Finally, I yanked the covers back and stormed out. I went next door to the spare bedroom and threw myself down on the bare mattress, giving it a few solid punches for good measure. "This fucking sucks, this fucking sucks, this fucking sucks!" I yelled. "This fucking sucks, this fucking sucks!" I said it over and over, like a mantra. And then, finally, the fury in my chest began to subside. It lost its insistence. After half an hour or so, I was able to go back to bed.

Two nights later—five days before I was supposed to return to the States—Samuel and I were lying in bed preparing to fall asleep when I told him, "I don't think I'm going to be able to get on that plane." Every time I envisioned the airport, I saw myself yanking my bags off the check-in scales and running back into Samuel's arms. I wanted to warn him.

Samuel pulled me close to him and held my head against his shoulder. "You don't have to," he said. "I'm not going to force you, Sharon. You can stay as long as you want." And it sounded like he really meant it.

So I started to think about what it would be like to stay longer—to spend another week or two weeks or four weeks in that seaside house. But as soon as I tried to picture it, I felt a deep conviction that that was not the right course. That I needed to go.

Samuel and I decided to go up to Paris for our last two days together. I packed my suitcases with all the items he'd brought for me from his dad's house. Everything was there: my pressure cooker, my DVDs, Joel Salatin's *Pastured Poultry Profits*. Samuel loaded everything into the car as I turned off the heat in the house and closed the blinds. I ran my hand over the light blue tablecloth, touching one last time this place where Samuel and I had shared so many intimate moments. These last few weeks, it seemed, had knit our souls together more tightly than ever before.

On our way to Paris, we stopped in Rennes, at a jewelry store. When Samuel had called off the wedding, I'd asked him to go to the jeweler's and try to get a refund for our wedding rings, which we'd ordered but never picked up. "I can't do that," he told me.

"Well, if we're not getting married," I said, "I want my money back."

"I can't do it," he insisted. And so he'd left the rings there, fully paid for.

Sometime during the first half of my visit, we'd discussed the matter again. "Why don't we keep the rings?" Samuel suggested.

"What am I going to do with a wedding ring?" I spat.

"They're not going to give us our money back," said Samuel. "And I can't see myself exchanging them for a watch. That wouldn't be right."

"Well, do what you want with mine," I said, "but I'm not keeping yours."

Nevertheless, by the time we were headed to Paris, my position had softened. I had dealt with the worst of my grief and anger, and I was no longer opposed to having something to remember our love by.

So we entered the same jewelry store we'd so happily visited as an engaged couple two months previously. The saleswoman took our names, retreated into the back room, and then returned with a little baggy that contained both of our wedding bands: plain yellow gold—one thick, one thin. She poured them into her palm and held them out to us. "*Essayez-les, s'il vous plaît.*" Please try them on.

"That's okay," I said. "We'll just take them."

"*Non, non, non,*" she insisted. "I need to make sure they're correctly sized."

Looking only for the quickest way to get out of there, Samuel and I took them from her. "Which hand?" asked Samuel, and I pointed to his left. The saleswoman smiled.

I slid my ring on, and it fit perfectly. I wasn't surprised by this, since we'd had our ring sizes measured in that very store just two months ago. Inexplicably, however, Samuel's ring turned out to be too big. It was so loose it would barely stay on his finger. The symbolism of this did not escape me.

"*Ça ne va pas du tout,*" said the saleswoman. "We'll have to resize that one for you."

"No, it's really all right," I said, and reached for the plastic baggy on the counter.

"*Il n'est pas question!*" she exclaimed and grabbed the baggy before I could get it. "I can't let you walk out with an incorrectly sized ring!"

"How long will it take?" I asked.

"Not long. A week. Maybe two."

"We'll take them the way they are," I insisted.

At that point, the saleswoman narrowed her eyes at us suspiciously, as though we might be trying to trick her into doing her job poorly. "*Dîtes-moi tout*," she said. Tell me everything.

At that point, candor seemed the only way to get her to leave us alone. "We're not getting married anymore," I told her. "So it really doesn't matter what size the rings are."

"Ah...." Her voice immediately lost its reprimanding tone. "Well then. Would you like me to put them in boxes for you? It's free."

Samuel and I looked at each other and nodded.

The rings disappeared into little white cases. "Would you like one bag or two?" she asked.

"One bag is fine," I said.

She wrapped the boxes in white tissue paper and gently placed them in a shiny pink and white gift bag. Its stripes reminded me of the bag of macaroons I'd once brought to Brittany. "There you are," she said.

Once Samuel and I were out of the jewelry store, ring bag in hand, the mood lightened considerably. We were in a mall, and as we neared the exit, we passed an Italian restaurant. "Do you want to get something to eat?" Samuel asked.

To save money, we usually just ate sandwiches when we were on the road, but for some reason this felt like a special occasion. We got ourselves a table for two, and I set the bag containing the rings right in the middle.

Samuel ordered a carafe of red wine.

"We should have a toast," I said, as Samuel filled our glasses.

He raised his and waited for me to speak.

I thought about it for a moment. How to pay tribute to everything wonderful we'd experienced together without being too sad or sentimental? I finally settled on the phrase, "May the future be as good as the past."

"*Oui*," agreed Samuel. And we clinked glasses and drank.

For the period of that lunch, I felt extremely strong. Triumphant, even. In the worst of worst situations, I was behaving like a truly self-reliant adult. And making sincerely cheerful predictions about the future.

The four-hour car ride to Paris brought me back to earth, however. Mile after monotonous mile of highway turned my thoughts to the hard reality that Samuel was choosing someone else instead of me. He was *abandoning* me, of his own free will. And that was not something I could be cheerful about. I got very quiet.

About halfway to Paris, we stopped at a travel plaza because Samuel needed a coffee. "Go on in," I said sullenly. "I'll wait here."

"Sharon, please come inside. We need to take a break from the car."

"I don't want to," I said. I no longer had the energy necessary to sit across a table from Samuel while he nursed his vending machine espresso.

"Please," he said again.

With a sigh, I got out of the car and followed him inside. When we sat down, I didn't say a word.

"What's wrong?" he asked.

"What's wrong?" I said, incredulous. "What's *wrong*? You're abandoning me! You're leaving me. I think I have the right to be sad about it."

Samuel sighed. Clearly he was exhausted, too. "I'm not leaving you, Sharon. If you're not leaving, I don't leave."

Well, that was not what he'd been saying for the last month. He'd been saying, "I think I'm going to have to be with her." Did he think that being with her was somehow compatible with not leaving me? I was too tired to ask for clarification. I was pretty sure Samuel meant his words to be comforting, so I just let myself be comforted. We went back to the car.

When we arrived in Paris, it was cold and rainy. We went directly to Samuel's sister's apartment, which she had left to us while she stayed at her boyfriend's down the street. It was a studio apartment, one room but spacious. It had a kitchenette at one end, a small wrought-iron table and a couch covered in Moroccan pillows in the middle, and, at the other end, a double bed and a set of wide casement windows looking out over the Canal de l'Ourcq. I moved restlessly from one end of the room to the other. Before arriving, I had finished all of my books from the used-book store, and I wouldn't be able to buy anything else until the shops opened at ten the next morning. I scanned Gwendoline's shelves, hoping to find something intriguing. On a shelf near the bed, my eye fell on a book called *Le bonheur d'être soi*. The Happiness of Being Oneself. I pulled it out and plopped down on the duvet.

The author, Moussa Nabati, was a therapist who focused on the way in which the circumstances of our early childhood affect our state of mind and behavior much later in life, even—or sometimes especially—if we can't consciously recall the events concerned. Nabati discussed some pretty extreme cases of manic and/or depressive adults, and though I wasn't quite at their level of disturbance, as I read the case histories, I did start to notice some similarities between these people and myself. For instance, Samuel had long pointed out to me that I had moments when I seemed deeply troubled but couldn't put words to my feelings or find any reasonable cause for them. Long before our recent problems—back when our relationship was relatively stress-free—I would sometimes start crying for no apparent reason. Usually it would be at bedtime. Samuel would try to comfort me, but I wouldn't be able to explain what was wrong, to him or to myself. Sometimes I would start feeling ambivalent about being close to Samuel. I would want to be comforted, but at the same time I would want to be away from him, as though somehow his physical proximity threatened my autonomy.

One night in our apartment in Massachusetts, I simply had to get up and leave the bed. I went down to the living room and sat for a while on the couch in the dark, trying to determine what was bothering me. I couldn't figure it out, but eventually I was able to go back to bed and fall asleep.

Another night that same year I felt so frustrated by this unexplained tension inside me that I actually shoved the lamp off my nightstand, sending it crashing to the floor and shattering the fluorescent bulb in a satisfying spray of sparks. Samuel looked at me aghast. "I don't know what's going on, but you're making me a little afraid," he said.

Another phenomenon, which I later came to believe was linked to the first one, was my frequent inability to put into words what I wanted or needed, even when I knew full well what that was, and even when it was something as inconsequential as wanting to show Samuel a new house plan I'd drawn. If I saw he was busy, I would hesitate to interrupt him, and yet, instead of either forgetting about it or just showing it to him anyway, I would sit or stand for a long time doing nothing, frozen between my desire to speak and my desire to keep silent. Eventually, Samuel would notice that something wasn't right. Sometimes he would notice it before I did, even though I was the one standing motionless in the middle of the room. "What's wrong?" he would ask. And, with a little more prompting, I could usually say that I just wanted to show him something. He would let me, and then we would both go happily on with our day, the issue seemingly resolved.

But this behavior kept recurring. In fact, it had happened several times during my present visit to France. And it was Nabati's books that suggested to me for the first time *why* it might be happening. I was an eldest child, with two younger siblings. I wasn't quite four years old when my first sister was born, and there must have been many moments in the early years of my life when I felt I needed attention and was told, or at least made to understand, that I couldn't have it, either because the baby had more pressing needs or because Mommy and Daddy were simply too tired. It would have been perfectly understandable for there to have been moments when this was really difficult for me but I nevertheless couldn't express my need for attention clearly, just because I was so young. The more I reflected on my current behavior with Samuel, the more it seemed to me exactly like an infantile reaction to need: standing around waiting for someone to notice my distress and come to my rescue.

But of course my circumstances had changed drastically since childhood. Now I *was* capable of saying what I needed. And now I was also aware that very few of these needs were needs of life or death, the way they had probably seemed in childhood. Once I realized, in reading Nabati's book, that my difficulty expressing my desires probably stemmed from a real childhood inability to do so, and realized that as an adult I *was* capable of expressing them and had no reason to fear doing so, a miraculous thing happened. Those childish reactions immediately disappeared.

The next morning, I wanted Samuel to do the breakfast dishes so I could get a shower before we went out for the day. In the past, I would have hesitated to ask him to do a favor like that. I would have just started doing the dishes, all the while talking about how I wanted to get going but still needed a shower, hoping he'd volunteer to finish the dishes for me. Instead of going through all of that this time, I simply asked Samuel, "Would you wash the dishes while I get a shower?" And the amazing thing was that, not only was Samuel happy to do them, but he actually seemed *appreciative* of my asking him, as though he was glad to be done with the guessing games.

I also realized while reading Nabati's book that I had long been trying to guess what *Samuel* needed, as though he too were concealing his desires from me. I realized that I'd been thinking almost constantly about how everything I did affected him and had been perpetually adjusting my behavior to what I imagined to be his wants. What was strange about this was that I had been burdening myself with desires that Samuel had never even expressed, and that it usually turned out he didn't actually *have*. I was projecting my *own* wants onto him. And sacrificing myself to them, probably in the unconscious hope that he would one day do the same for me.

But after I realized that I was fully capable of expressing my needs, I also realized that Samuel was capable of expressing his. And that he usually did! Most of the burdens I'd placed on myself in the name of a loving, altruistic relationship—doing unto others as I would have them do unto me—were artificial and unnecessary.

When I finally trusted Samuel to tell me when he needed something, the feeling of freedom was immense. That first morning in Paris, I was able to stay in bed an extra two hours reading Nabati's book and not worry about whether Samuel, who was reading his own book at the table nearby, was silently wishing I would get up. I had the amazing revelation that, if he wanted me to get up, he would say so! And since he never did, I got up when I *felt* like getting up, not when I felt like I had to in order to avoid seeming selfish. It was at that point that I asked Samuel to do the dishes. And if he did them so gladly, perhaps it was in part because we'd just spent such a relaxing morning, each completely absorbed in our own pursuits.

When we left the apartment, we decided to make the rounds of our favorite Parisian bookstores and cafés. It felt just like old times, taking in the town and taking our time. We browsed Gibert Joseph as well as some of the more academic bookstores in the neighborhood. We sipped coffee and nibbled pastries and talked about coincidences and the meaning of life. We made the most of that day, and the next day as well.

And then it was our last night together.

I suggested to Samuel that we go back to the restaurant where we'd had our very first date, the one where I'd told him about my mom's email and we'd pondered the nature of spirituality. "I don't know if that's a good idea," Samuel said.

It was true that we didn't normally try to repeat experiences that were brilliant the first time, and that this particular occasion might be ripe for emotional disaster. But I was feeling unexpectedly positive on our last night together: defiant, even. I'd be damned if I let a little thing like the prospect of breaking up ruin this chance to celebrate all the wonderful moments Samuel and I had shared! "How about this?" I said. "Let's walk by the restaurant, and if the table we ate at in 2007 is free, we'll go in. If not, we'll go someplace else."

This seemed to appeal to Samuel's belief in the guiding hand of the universe, so we crossed the street toward the restaurant and were about to walk to the other side of the entrance so we could get a good view of the interior when a waiter put his arm out to us. "*Bonsoir! Entrez à l'intérieur où il fait chaud!*"

"Should we go in?" I asked Samuel. From where we were standing, we couldn't see whether our table was available or not.

"*Pourquoi pas?*" he said. Why not?

And so we followed the waiter inside, and he seated us at a little table in the corner. From there, we looked over the dining room and tried to determine where we had been sitting in May 2007. "I think it was there," I said, pointing to an empty table by the window.

"But wasn't it a square table?" asked Samuel. "Like that one?" He pointed to another table by the window, one that was pushed up next to a column, and at which a couple was sitting.

"I guess they've rearranged," I said, shrugging. "Our table from 2007 doesn't really exist anymore. Maybe that's appropriate." I smiled and raised my glass. "To the future."

We had brought our rings with us to the restaurant, their little boxes tucked carefully into Samuel's bookbag, but the moment never seemed quite right for exchanging them. The venue wasn't private enough. And the restaurant was too loud. Right behind us, eight Brazilians were very vocally celebrating a birthday.

So we waited until we got back to the apartment. We settled ourselves on the bed in front of the great big window overlooking the canal. I took Samuel's ring from its box, and he took mine.

"We should put them on our right hands," I said. "Since they're not wedding bands anymore."

"Wedding rings go on the left hand?" Samuel asked, uncertain yet again. This time, I was reminded of the very first day I'd met him, in Nancy nine years before. I'd put my mother's ring on my left ring finger to signal to him that I was an engaged woman. Obviously, that had been wasted effort. For a whole bunch of reasons.

"Yes," I said. "Although I think in Israel they put them on the right hand." I mentioned this because Samuel and I had always joked about our being Jewish. Neither of us were ethnically or religiously Jewish, but both of our names were Jewish, and we'd been brought together by my friend Shira, an actual Jew. What was more, we'd spent two years at Brandeis, a Jewish-sponsored university. And in our various world travels we'd often talked longingly about visiting the Holy Land. Upon returning from a trip, we would tell each other, "Next year in Jerusalem."

"What should we say?" asked Samuel, holding my ring in his hand.

I took the ring I was giving him and held it to the tip of his right ring finger. "*Ceci n'est pas une promesse,*" I said. "*C'est un symbole de tout l'amour que je t'ai offert.*" I slid the ring on, loose as it was.

Samuel slid my ring onto my finger while saying the same words: "This ring is not a promise. It's a symbol of all the love I've given you."

We clasped hands and sat quietly for a moment. The silence in the room had something of the sacred about it. Then, in a gentle, tender voice, Samuel asked, "Do you want to make love?"

I thought about it carefully. About what I really wanted. "No, I don't think so," I said. "I feel a little sad."

So Samuel leaned his back against the headboard of the bed and pulled his legs up toward him. I draped my arms over them and rested my chin on his knees. I gazed at his face, trying to fill my mind so full of this moment that I'd be able to return to it in memory whenever I wanted.

"Are you sure you don't want to make love?" Samuel asked again a few minutes later, likely spurred by the intensity of my gaze.

I shook my head. "I'm not in the mood right now. I'm not sure why, but I'm not."

Eventually, we got up to brush our teeth and put on our pajamas. Once we were beneath the covers, we snuggled up to each other. "This was a beautiful day," said Samuel.

"Yes, it was."

"Whatever happens, Sharon, I love you."

"I love you, too," I assured him.

And then, just as clearly as I had previously felt that I didn't want to make love, I now felt that I did.

Our love making had always been beautiful, starting with the very first time almost four years ago, when I'd finally told Samuel I was ready. We'd just come back from the election weekend in Brittany, and when our carpool dropped us off on the outskirts of Paris, we went down into the metro together. We'd been together every night of our first three nights as a couple, and as much as I wanted to spend this night with Samuel as well, I figured he probably expected us to go our separate ways now that we were back in the city. I started looking at the map of the metro lines, trying to figure out which train to take back to my dorm at the ENS, but Samuel interrupted my thoughts. "We can take the 1 to the 7," he said, tapping his stop. In his mind, there was apparently no doubt that we were going home together.

Back in his apartment, we fell quickly into bed. Samuel began kissing me, and I felt even more strongly than on previous nights a desire to be utterly and wholly his. The only thing that was holding me back was my uncertainty about the seriousness of our relationship. I was leaving France in a week and a half. Did Samuel see that as a natural ending point for our relationship? Was he assuming this would just be a fling, and that's why he was so eager to spend every night together?

The desire to make love with him was so intense that it pushed me to ask the question that had been on my mind all weekend. "I'm only in Paris for ten more days," I said. "What are you thinking about the future?"

"I'm trying not to dwell on that too much," he replied, immediately causing my heart to drop. But then he continued, "As soon as I do, I start thinking about buying plane tickets for the States."

That second line was all I needed to hear. I didn't need to know that he was *definitely* coming to the U.S. Just that he considered it a live possibility. When he began kissing my neck, I whispered into his ear, "*Faisons l'amour.*" Let's make love.

"Are you sure?" he asked.

His concern only made me want him more. "*Oui*," I assured him. "I want you to make love to me."

My evangelical sex education had taught me to expect pain, tears, and the sense of having lost something priceless and irretrievable, but I didn't care. This was the moment I had chosen. This was the man I wanted to share it with. And I guess I chose well, because none of the evangelicals' predictions came true. Making love with Samuel didn't feel like anything *close* to a loss. It felt perfect. Beautiful. And extraordinarily empowering. When I went to the toilet afterward and noticed a small amount of blood, I simply felt pleased. I sat there for a moment, watching the dawn light creep over the sky outside the bathroom window. Now I was a woman. Now I was capable of anything.

Three and a half years later, our love making was just as powerful. And, for the first time, it also felt completely pure. On this night, as we were saying goodbye, our love felt wholly untainted by either selfishness or sacrifice. I was following my own desires completely while at the same time wishing with all my heart that Samuel would have the fulfillment of his, whatever they turned out to be.

When Samuel fell asleep afterward, I didn't feel lonely, as sometimes happened. I felt a deep sense of peace. I had finally begun to find myself in the revelations of the last couple of weeks. I had learned that the source of my happiness was not external to me, in Samuel or in anyone or anything else. My happiness came from knowing who I was and allowing that self to express itself. My happiness, I had learned, came from the very deepest wells of the universe. Wells that would never run dry.

I realized, too, that I'd been waiting for a long time for the right man to come along and marry me so that I could finally start building the home and farm I'd always wanted. For the last couple of years, I'd been waiting for Samuel to be ready to settle down before I could devote myself fully to my dreams. That had made me feel like a caged animal. The year before last, he'd insisted we spend the whole summer at the beach house instead of the farm, and I'd gone stir-crazy. Even long walks in the nearby fields couldn't make up for the lack of productive physical labor. "I need my hands in the dirt," I told him. "I need something to *do*. This is a huge waste of a summer!" As many times as I'd explained these feelings to Samuel, I felt he never really understood their gravity.

Now I knew it was time for me to do what I'd always wanted to do, with or without him. As I lay in bed on what could certainly have been the saddest night of my life, I imagined going home to Virginia, buying a few acres of land and starting to build a house—the house I'd been designing for as long as I could remember. I pictured myself living out of a pickup truck and a camping trailer. With a dog and maybe some goats and chickens for company. The thought of it made me cry tears of joy. I fell asleep that night with those images firmly planted in my soul, a powerful kernel of hope.

The next morning, Samuel and I made ourselves a light breakfast before we left for the airport. The sun had yet to come up as we sat at the little metal table next to the kitchenette and spread butter and jam on what remained of the previous day's baguette. We sipped cups of Samuel's high-octane coffee.

"I have two things to tell you," I said. "First, please tell your family not to worry about me. I'm doing well." I smiled and hoped he saw how true this was. "The second thing is that I know I can't wait for you in planning the next part of my life. I *shouldn't* do that, and it's not what you want either—for me to wait for you to decide if you're ever coming back."

I put my hand on Samuel's. "*Je ne t'attends pas. Mais mon coeur te sera toujours ouvert.*" I'm not going to wait for you, but my heart will still be open.

Chapter ELEVEN

Samuel drove me to the airport. We shared another cup of coffee, and then Samuel walked me to security. We stood for a long while just looking at each other. When I was finally able to gather the courage, I said, "*Au revoir.*"

"Do you mean that?" Samuel asked. "That we'll see each other again?"

"I'm not ruling it out," I said. "But it's more up to you than me."

I hugged him fiercely then, tears streaming from the corners of my eyes. Afterward, he kissed me and then stood back to look at me once more. I could see two wet tracks gliding down his own cheeks. "*Au revoir, Shahone.*"

Strangely, I cried less than at some of our other goodbyes, when we'd only been parting for a month or two. Something about the ring on my finger made the trip through security and passport control bearable. This idea that, although Samuel and I weren't married, and although he might be on his way to marrying someone else, we had declared our love for each other in a formal and enduring way. A way that I was carrying on my hand. For the moment, that was enough to keep me in one piece.

On the plane, all my sleepless nights in Brittany finally caught up with me. I lowered my seatback, pulled the wings of the headrest around my temples, and slept most of the way through the transatlantic flight. Some part of me, perhaps, knew that I was going to need all my strength for what was coming next. After all, it was one thing to say goodbye. Actually moving on to the next stage of my life, a stage without Samuel...that was something else entirely.

But, by the time the plane touched down in Pennsylvania, I felt refreshed. When I boarded my flight to Washington, it was starting to get dark outside, but I was wide awake. I played with the ring on my finger. I watched the other passengers. Most of them looked like business people: stockbrokers, analysts, lobbyists. They probably did this trip several times per month, if not per week. They seemed in surprisingly good spirits as they chatted amongst themselves.

Finally, my mind wandered back to Paris, and Samuel. And I found myself having a vision. Not the religious kind. More like a vivid daydream. It was very similar to something I'd been seeing in my head on and off for the past several weeks. I would be in Samuel's sister's apartment in Paris, and in the double bed, by the windows overlooking the canal, would be Samuel...and Her. They'd be snuggled under the duvet together, gazing into each other's eyes, smiling and laughing. Meanwhile, I'd be standing off to the side in the little hallway that led to the bathroom, feeling alone and forgotten.

Up until a couple of months ago, I'd believed that the only reason there could ever be occasion for jealousy in a relationship was if one of the partners was a real jerk. A decent human being in a good relationship might sometimes be attracted to people other than their partner, but I believed they would always write that attraction off as a passing thing and never allow it to make the person they loved uneasy. Honestly, I'd thought that jealousy was the sort of thing that, if I chose my partner wisely, I would never have to grapple with.

And yet there it was: smack in the middle of a relationship that by every other indication had been extremely healthy and loving. And there *I* was, finding it next to impossible to just jump ship. Because I *knew* Samuel. And because I knew that he would never have put me through all this if it wasn't serious. If he didn't have valid doubts about marrying me. It wasn't an ideal situation by any means, but I couldn't fault Samuel for feeling what he felt or having the questions that he had. If I had found myself in a similar situation, I would have wanted understanding, not anger. And so I felt I owed it to Samuel, for all we'd experienced together, for all the beautiful moments we'd shared. I owed it to Samuel to love him. Not to hate him.

Nevertheless, the jealousy was something I was forced to reckon with. I could love Samuel all I wanted, but when I thought of him with this other woman, the fact that I loved him only made the knot in my stomach grow tighter.

While reading Arnaud Desjardins' book, I'd been surprised by the number of times he used romantic jealousy as an example of an unpleasant feeling we need to learn to face and accept. Desjardins wrote in *Les chemins de sagesse* that, if I felt jealousy, it meant something was amiss with *me*. My jealousy was an indication that *I* still had growing to do. That I still had crucial things to learn about love. And, honestly, I felt he might be right.

But even after I accepted that I needed to deal with my jealousy, I wasn't sure what to do with it. At times, my feelings of jealousy manifested as a very physical sense of revulsion, and this revulsion seemed entirely out of my control. I could acknowledge it and not run away from it, but the vision of Samuel with this other woman returned over and over. I tried not to avoid it. I tried to watch it carefully to see what it might teach me. But it was painful. It made me ache from loneliness. And anger. And fear. And all my best intentions didn't seem to produce any progress. Until the plane ride home.

The vision I had on the way from Philadelphia to Washington was very similar to the others I'd had, but there was one fundamental difference. There was no longer a third person in the scene. There was no longer a figure representing my lonely, neglected self. Instead of standing off to one side watching Samuel and this other woman, I now found myself, against all expectation, *identifying* with them. For some reason, as I watched the imaginary scene this time, I felt their joy. I saw their smiles and heard their laughter, and I participated in the happiness they felt in finding each other after so many years. In fact, I actually felt as if I were *giving* them this gift of togetherness, and rejoicing in their enjoyment of it.

How on earth had this happened? It wasn't like I'd been trying to make myself see the situation this way. I hadn't been saying any sort of mantra to myself, trying to identify with *Her* point of view. And yet, somehow, that evening, the vision transformed itself. By some unconscious emotional alchemy, jealousy metamorphosed into empathy.

Over the next few days, as I adjusted to being back home, I reflected on this unexpected transformation. And I began to suspect that my sudden ability to accept the idea of Samuel's being happy with someone else had come about as a result of the recent revolution I'd experienced in my perception of myself. When I viewed myself as hurting and abandoned, picturing the two of them happy together was acutely painful. But, when I saw myself as someone whole, as someone with great internal love and strength, picturing them happy only increased that feeling of love. My feelings toward others, I realized, were to a large extent a reflection of my feelings towards myself.

Now that I was back in the States, I knew that one of my most important tasks was to take myself seriously, and in particular to take my desires seriously. So, even though I was once again living in my parents' house, I made sure to allow myself as much solitude as I wanted. In the evenings, while they watched TV, I sat alone in my room—reading, thinking, and meditating. Sitting in the presence of this newly discovered self.

It didn't take me many such evenings to realize that this self had desires that went beyond building a farm full of plants and animals. Almost immediately, I had the itch to start another writing project. During the month I'd spent in France, I'd finished the French novel I'd been writing for the last three years, the one I'd begun just a few months after Samuel and I started dating. It had seemed appropriate to complete that project just as my relationship with Samuel was drawing to a close. At the end of the novel, I had the French guy, whose name was Nicolas, decide to go back to his American girlfriend. And I named the book *Je reviens*: I'll Be Back. I wrote in the dedication that the book was "[f]or my own Nicolas, even if he doesn't return."

Thinking about where to turn my creative energies next, I was drawn to the idea of the memoir I'd started five years ago: a chronicle of my experiences growing up in the Southern Baptist Church and losing my faith at a Christian college. I'd worked on it during the year I'd lived at the ENS in Paris, and I'd managed to bring it almost current, to the time of my arrival there. But I didn't know where to go with it after that. I could have written a story that culminated in my decision to abandon the sexual mores of my youth and live happily ever after as an atheist, but something about that didn't ring true. Or at least didn't inspire me to write. I think I knew that I was still searching for something, still waiting for something else to happen. To borrow a line from U2, I still hadn't found what I was looking for.

But now, with everything that had happened in the wake of Samuel's announcement that he couldn't marry me, I knew I had found it. Or at least that I was hot on its trail. And that gave me something to write about. A story that I was frankly very excited to tell.

The only thing discouraging me was the fact that I hated the tone of my previous writing. I'd begun the memoir because I couldn't help myself, because I had a deep need to tell the story of my struggles with God and the church. But I'd never liked the *way* I told the story. The hundred or so pages I had in my notebook seemed stilted and self-conscious. Reading them over again, I knew that writing a longer memoir in that voice would be a waste of time. It wouldn't be something that could find its way to the rest of the world through publication. And I desperately wanted it to find its way out into the world, to touch and encourage other people, the way I had been touched by countless memoirs over the years.

It was while I was debating how to proceed that my mom showed me a book she'd been reading during my month in France. It was a small hardback library book, maybe two hundred pages long, called *The Right to Write*. "It's not really about *how* to write," she said. "It's about why we shouldn't be afraid to write. Julia Cameron insists that creative expression is something we all have a right to, no matter how good or bad we are at it."

Just a couple of days later, my mom told me about something she'd seen in another book: *This Is Your Brain on Music* by Daniel Levitin. "They've done studies on what separates world-class performers from people who are just very good at music or mediocre," she said, "and they've found that all of the people considered world-class have put in at least ten thousand hours of practice. They looked at people who were world-class in other areas, too—sports, painting, math, whatever—and the same thing was true. The crucial difference between people who had some skill and people who performed at an outstanding level was the amount of time they'd already devoted to doing that thing. Initial aptitude mattered much less than *practice*."

I wasn't sure how "world-class" was defined by the people who did these studies, and I was skeptical about there being any exact amount of time, like ten thousand hours, that it would take to become world-class at just anything. I mean, could it really take ten thousand hours to become a world-class pencil sharpener? Then again, to really be considered world-class, you'd probably have to do some pretty creative sharpening....

But, regardless of how this research applied to other occupations, I was very encouraged to hear that ten thousand hours was the approximate amount of time it had taken writers and musicians to rise to the tops of their fields. Because, even though ten thousand hours seemed overwhelming, it gave me an excellent explanation as to why my writing wasn't yet where I wanted it to be: I hadn't practiced enough. But, if I kept at it, I could expect to keep improving. And, actually, when I stopped to think about it, in the three years since I'd last worked on my memoir, I *had* written both a novel and a dissertation. That ought to make some sort of difference.

"Ten thousand hours is only three hours a day for ten years," my mom pointed out in encouragement. Again, that sounded like a lot. But then I thought about the fact that I'd been writing stories and plays since I was seven years old. That was twenty-two years ago. Ten thousand hours spread over twenty-two years was less than an hour and a half each day. Could I have averaged something close to that, given how intensively I'd worked on my novels and screenplays during my teenage years? Even my hours of writing academic philosophy could probably count for half credit. Maybe I was approaching ten thousand hours now! And maybe, in the time it took me to finish my memoir, I would cross the magic threshold.

On Thanksgiving Day, I officially decided to reembark on my memoir project. I had a stack of brand new Clairefontaine notebooks from Gibert Joseph waiting on the shelf that sat at the head of my bed, and when I crawled under the covers that night, it was with the intention of getting up early the next morning to start writing. However, as I lay there waiting to fall asleep, I couldn't stop thinking about possible opening lines. I ended up lying awake until well past midnight turning over phrases in my head. Finally, I turned on my lamp and pulled a notebook off the shelf. The glossy green cover was still stiff from newness. Skipping the first crisp white page to leave room for a title, at the top of the second page I wrote two sentences that had finally crystallized in my head: "Just a couple of months past my twenty-ninth birthday, I believed that all my dreams had come true. I was engaged to a man I loved so much I sometimes cried from happiness just being near him." It wasn't clever. It wasn't affected. It wasn't self-conscious. It was simply honest. It felt like my own voice, translated to the page. By the time I fell asleep in the early hours of the morning, I had written an entire three-page prologue.

After that, I began every day with writing. I woke up while it was still dark and installed myself at my parents' long mahogany dining table with a mug of hot jasmine tea, my notebook, and a plain ballpoint pen. Back when I'd been writing my French novel, I'd thought that writing three pages a day was the most I was capable of. After that, I felt too tired to do my best work. But, once I got into the rhythm of the memoir, three pages a day became my minimum. I was consistently writing five or six. And then eight or nine. The first day I wrote twelve pages in a stretch, I was exhausted and thought I would never be able to do it again. But a week later, I had a day where I wrote fifteen pages. Ten became normal. And even though I only "required" myself to write six days a week, I often found myself writing on Sundays, too. Because writing, for me, was not primarily work. Every time I sat down with my notebook and pen, I was rewarded with some fascinating new memory or some new way of looking at my experiences. Writing was an adventure—a peculiarly comforting one. And it was a very cheap form of therapy.

The time I didn't spend writing I spent in other activities that interested me: reading, drawing, knitting, and searching Craigslist for land, pickup trucks, and camping trailers. After only a week of this new routine—a routine in which the dominant factor was my deep interest and involvement in everything I was doing—I noticed a curious thing. Ever since I'd been very young, no matter what I'd happened to be doing, even if it was just playing with LEGOs alone in my room, I had always done this thing where I imagined myself showing off my work to someone else. "You're so creative, industrious, and smart!" my imaginary audience would exclaim. I'd been manufacturing this imaginary praise for so long that I'd seen my original audience—made up of parents and teachers—get replaced by an imaginary future husband who, among other things, was especially impressed by my cooking. I'd been fully aware of this little psychological tic, but I figured it was only natural, since we all want the approval of others. However, just a week after beginning regular work on my memoir, I realized that this imaginary chorus had evaporated. I was going about the activities of my day as usual, but for the first time I heard no imaginary lovers or parents or teachers or friends expressing awe or admiration.

I speculated about the reason for this. I wondered whether, previously, to justify doing something, I'd needed to believe that others approved of my doing it. Had I thought that doing something just because *I* wanted to wasn't good enough? Certainly I'd been taught, growing up, that my own desires should be subservient to God's. And, somewhat less explicitly, I'd been taught that they ought to serve what society expected and valued (for instance, getting good grades in school).

Now, though, it seemed that my own approval was enough for me. But why? Maybe it was because *now I finally had it*. Now I was finally pursuing my deepest, most personal dreams: to be a writer and a homesteader. I didn't need any imaginary praise because, for the first time, I myself believed wholeheartedly in what I was doing.

Nevertheless, I wasn't invulnerable to detours.

In late November, I decided to browse the online job listings for philosophers. I knew that all the application deadlines had already passed, so it wasn't like I was intending to apply. I was just curious, and maybe looking for some additional confirmation of my decision to leave academia. The previous year there hadn't been a single philosophy opening in the mid-Atlantic region that fit my rank and specialization. I figured that, if things were similar this year, that would be a pretty good sign that my decision to leave academia had been a wise one. And it would be an easy way to justify that decision to others.

I wasn't expecting what I found: an advertisement for an opening at James Madison University. Not only was JMU in Virginia, and in the part of the state I loved most—the mountains—but it was located in Harrisonburg, a city whose name I recognized from my years of attending a Mennonite church in New York. I knew Harrisonburg as the home of Eastern Mennonite University and a whole community of progressive Mennonites concerned about pacifism and social justice. I couldn't think of any corner of Virginia I'd rather settle in.

But that wasn't all. The job opening at JMU was in precisely my specialty: metaethics. And to top it all off, the advertisement stated that the hiring process had been delayed. Applications weren't due until December 17. Still three weeks away.

Many of the spiritual self-help books I'd been reading (such as Julia Cameron's *The Right to Write*) encouraged the belief that, when we take the risk of moving in a new and worthwhile direction, the universe helps us out by providing perfectly timed opportunities. Having been with Samuel for three and a half years, I was no stranger to this line of thought. But I realized now, thinking back, that even before dating Samuel, I'd had some striking experiences along these lines. All of them, strangely enough, were connected to France.

After my first study-abroad experience in college, I didn't go back to France for four years. And then, rather abruptly, I felt the need to do so. That's when I was in my third year of graduate school and planned the trip to Paris for my Christmas break. I was so determined to go that I bought my plane tickets before I'd even figured out where I was going to stay, and before I'd even told my roommate in New York that I was going. A friend of hers from Turkey was coming to stay at our apartment over Christmas break, and when I eventually mentioned that I was going to be in Paris at that time, she exclaimed, "That's where my friend lives!"

"I thought he was Turkish," I said.

"He is, but he's studying in Paris right now. He has an apartment in La Défense. If you want, I'm sure he'd let you stay at his place while he's here."

It turned out that he was more than happy to lend me his Paris apartment for ten days. But, as amazingly convenient as that synchronicity was, the story didn't end there. My roommate's friend sent me directions to his apartment and mailed his spare key to my parents' house in Virginia, where I was spending Christmas before flying out on December twenty-seventh. But Christmas came and went, and the key didn't arrive. I was suddenly imagining myself lugging my suitcase around the streets of Paris, trying to find a hotel room that wouldn't eat up half my life savings. I frantically emailed the guy, who in turn called my cell phone. "I'm so sorry," he said. "I wish I could just ask the concierge to let you in, but I'm not really supposed to loan my student apartment."

All I could think was that there had to be a solution. It would just be too ridiculous to be deprived of my free place to stay in Paris because a key got lost in the mail!

"I'm coming to New York tomorrow," said the Turkish guy. "Will you still be there?"

"No," I said despairingly. "I'm in Virginia already. I fly out of DC tomorrow afternoon. You're already in the States?"

"Yes, I'm in Duke. Visiting my girlfriend."

"Duke University? In North Carolina?"

"Yes."

I thought about driving down there. It was only four hours away. But then a light went on. "How are you getting to New York?" I asked.

"The train. Why?"

Back when I'd been in college, I'd ridden Amtrak back and forth from Virginia to Philly to visit Daniel, and I knew that all the trains heading up the coast from North Carolina passed through the city just thirty minutes from my parents' house. So, the next day, I waited on the platform. Finally, a train pulled into the station, and a little ways down the platform, I saw a dark-haired, Turkish-looking young man step off. I ran straight to him, he dropped the key in my hand, and before I'd even had a chance to feel relieved, he was back on the train, chugging off into the distance.

At the time, I'd considered this a stroke of very good luck. I'd considered it lucky, too, that Samuel happened to have returned to France from Canada a few months previously and that I got the chance to meet his family and see their farm. And I considered it even more amazingly good luck when, a month later, I was looking for a way to get back to France for a longer stay and one of my professors informed me, without knowing anything about my interest, that the philosophy department had been vainly trying to find someone who would be willing to study in Paris.

It wasn't until five years later, after all my recent spiritual experiences, that I realized something deeper might have been at work, especially when I considered that those synchronicities had made possible two of the most significant relationships in my life: my relationship to Samuel and my relationship to France. Having recently mulled over these providential coincidences, I was very alert to the possible significance of the perfect job opportunity at JMU that seemed to have been thrust into my lap.

Since having decided not to apply for philosophy jobs the previous fall, I'd had no serious second thoughts about leaving academia, but now I wondered if I could have been wrong to abandon philosophy so quickly. Was God and/or the Universe trying to gently steer me back? Maybe one of the reasons for my breakup with Samuel had been to keep me from abandoning my professional career. Certainly the extra income would be nice. The land I'd been looking at buying near my parents' house cost more than I'd anticipated. To leave enough money for building a house, I was having to look at more marginal land, with less acreage. However, if I signed on for a few more years of full-time work, I could save enough extra cash to buy the kind of property I'd originally envisioned: ten acres, half in woods and half in pasture, with a stream running through it. Maybe this job at JMU was meant to be?

I immediately emailed the Director of Placement at NYU's Philosophy Department, who had told me that he'd be happy to help me apply for jobs after my fellowship at Brandeis was up. With his enthusiastic encouragement, I embarked on the weeks-long process of assembling all the necessary documents: resume, cover letter, writing samples, references, teaching portfolio.

I also needed to compose a page-long statement of my future research interests. It had been a long time since I'd had *any* interests with regard to philosophy. It wasn't easy to make my research program sound exciting to potential employers when it didn't even sound exciting to me. Nevertheless, I pulled something together and, when I handed the package to my mom to look over, realized that it actually looked quite impressive.

"Oh, no!" I told her. "They might offer me the job!"

That should probably have been my first clue.

But I was distracted by another coincidence. I had to send my completed application to the NYU Philosophy Department, where the placement director would insert my recommendation letters and mail the whole package to JMU before December 17. I was preparing to write NYU's address on the envelope when it hit me that I didn't *need* to mail it, because I was going to New York in person in just a few days. Somehow, until then, I hadn't made the connection between my application and the fact that I'd been making plans to visit a couple of my friends from college, one of whom now lived in Manhattan. It just so happened that I had independently planned a trip to the city where I needed to deposit my application, in the very week when I needed to do it. It once again seemed meant to be. And so, without further reflection, I stuck the manila envelope containing my application materials into my backpack and jumped on the bus for New York.

Along the way, I listened to a CD Samuel had recently mailed me. Since my return to the States, Samuel had not only been sending me daily emails, he'd also started mailing me weekly packages, with books or music or sometimes just newspaper clippings with important events highlighted and his commentary written in the margins. One of the recent packages contained a CD by Jean-Jacques Goldman, one of France's most beloved songwriters. The album, titled *Entre gris clair et gris foncé* (Between light gray and dark gray), was from 1987, and Samuel told me he wanted me to hear it because it was the sound of his teenage years, the years he'd been having such a difficult time explaining to me. Of the entire album, the song that stuck out to me most was "*Là-bas*." It was a duet between a man and a woman, where the man says over and over that he needs to leave, and the woman pleads with him to stay. She says it's too dangerous where he wants to go, but he says he either has to go or risk losing himself. In the end, he says he has no choice.

While listening to that song, I thought about the need that both Samuel and I had to be free and to follow our missions in life however we understood them. I thought, particularly, of Samuel's frequent comment that he wished he was a monk. Suddenly, I understood it much better than in the past, since I was now going through a "monk" period of my own, a time when all I wanted was to be left alone to read and write. And I understood much better Samuel's previous frustration at not having the freedom to focus on the ideas that he was passionate about exploring.

These thoughts were still fresh in my mind when the bus approached an overpass. The New Jersey Turnpike carried us under a bridge on which two lone words had been written in graffiti. Actually, it was a single word, repeated. The bridge read, "MONK MONK." And I thought, *One is Samuel, one is me.*

An hour or so later, the bus dropped me on a street corner in midtown Manhattan. I gathered my suitcase from the undercarriage and looked around to get my bearings. Immediately I saw a street sign just a few yards away. The bus had dropped us on the corner of 33rd Street. I dug my camera out of my bag and snapped a picture.

Not ten minutes later, I was walking south on Fifth Avenue toward my friend Carl's office when I passed a place called "Le Bar Breton," between 29th and 28th Streets. I'm sure it had been there for a long time, but I'd lived for four years in Manhattan and this was the first I'd ever seen it. I knew then, without a shadow of a doubt, that this trip to New York was going to be very important.

The bus had arrived in Manhattan in the late afternoon—too late, I told myself, to rush down to NYU with my application. So, instead of heading to Washington Square, I found a coffee shop on Sixth Avenue where I could work on my memoir while I waited for Carl to get out of work and my friend Alicia to arrive on the train from her home in Connecticut.

The next morning, I decided it *still* wasn't a good time to deliver the application. Alicia would only be in town for one day. We should spend it doing fun things, not schlepping to NYU. So we dedicated the morning to Alicia's hobby of letterboxing, scouring Manhattan looking for the little rubber ink stamps that other letterboxers had hidden in odd places, like inside a decorative cookie tin in the window display of a Chelsea bakery. Then we spent the afternoon at The Strand, a gigantic used bookstore on Broadway just a few blocks north of NYU.

I spent most of my time in the store searching for a Christmas present to send to Samuel. At first, I didn't have much luck, but after thirty minutes or so, my eyes fell on a copy of Deepak Chopra's *How to Know God*. I was a little wary of Chopra, since he seemed to make an awful lot of money from his New Age teachings and to be very popular among movie stars—not people to whom I usually turned for spiritual advice. At the same time, I remembered that one of my professors at Messiah College had assigned our philosophy of science class an excerpt from Chopra. And I knew Samuel liked him, since a couple of years ago he'd urged me to read Chopra's book on synchronicities.

So I took *How to Know God* off the shelf and flipped through it. "Life looks meaningless when you have worn out old responses, old realities, and an old version of God," wrote Chopra. "To bring God back, we have to follow new, even strange responses wherever they lead us." It was astounding. This book seemed to be about *exactly* the kind of spiritual transformation I was currently experiencing. Chopra described seven spiritual stages, and the seven different "Gods" we believe in at those stages. I recognized myself as having recently moved from belief in the rules-obsessed, guilt-inducing God of Stage Two—the one who'd pushed me to abandon theism altogether—to belief in the peaceful God of Stage Three and then on to the God of pure acceptance and love of Stage Four.

A couple of weeks ago—just a few days after I'd stopped needing an imaginary audience for all my activities— I'd been climbing into bed, thinking excitedly about getting up the next day to write, when suddenly I'd been overcome by a very intense feeling, a feeling that I couldn't describe in any other way than as love. I wasn't looking for it. I wasn't meditating or praying or reading the Bible. I was just getting ready for bed when suddenly I *felt* it: an overwhelming degree of compassion—even adoration—directed straight at me. *God loves me*, I thought, with absolute conviction. It was exactly what I'd been aching to feel every time I'd prayed my tearful college prayers. It was absolutely stunning.

Standing in an aisle of The Strand reading Chopra, I finally began to understand why it had taken me so long to have this experience. Chopra wrote that the key to finding the loving, accepting God of Stage Four is *self*-acceptance. When we love ourselves, when we don't doubt our own inner voice, then we feel loved by God. God and the Self, I think Chopra would say, are not really two separate entities. That certainly wasn't an idea I was used to, having grown up an evangelical Christian, but given my recent experiences, it didn't seem that crazy.

When I got back to Carl's apartment that evening, I looked back in my journal and saw that, the day before I'd had my intense experience of divine love, I'd written this: "'I *should* do this.' 'I *should* do that.' It's time to give up the should's and be myself. If I am something of a free spirit…so be it! That's who I've always been, and I'm not likely to be happy being anything else!"

It had finally struck me that I could find happiness by ceasing to put all of my energy into fitting into other people's ideas of what I ought to be—for instance, a well-dressed career woman who remembered every metaethics article ever written and wrote impeccably reasoned and wholly unemotional essays. Instead, I could simply accept that, whoever I was and however my life turned out, things were okay, and that was the way they were meant to be.

This attitude had given me a new perspective on all kinds of things, including something that had happened to me in grad school. Every spring, the philosophy faculty at NYU held a meeting to discuss the progress of the PhD students. My first year there, my advisor had come by my office after the meeting to let me know what they'd said about me. "Elaine says your work is erratic," he told me. Then he tapped the doorframe and went on down the hall. I wasn't entirely sure what 'erratic' meant, but it felt devastating.

Now, looking back, I had a different perspective. Since it was near the beginning of the semester, and this was only my first class with Elaine, I knew that the remark had to have been elicited by an oral presentation I'd given, in which I'd discussed some of my very new, only half-formed ideas. I remembered that I had purposely taken the risk to talk about those new ideas, even though they weren't fully worked out or easy to explain. And, in the end, it had been those ideas that became the thesis of my award-winning dissertation. Maybe, instead of "Your work is erratic," I should have heard, "You risk discussing exciting new theories."

In any case, it had now become clear to me that I would do the world the most good by being myself, however erratic I might actually turn out to be. And it was this change in attitude that appeared to have opened the floodgates of divine love. Chopra had hit the nail on the head.

My last full day in New York was the day after I found Chopra's book. It was also the only day left for me to deliver my application materials to NYU. When I woke up that morning, Alicia had already returned to Connecticut and Carl had left for work. In the empty apartment, I made myself some oatmeal and tea and sat down with them at the little wooden table that stood just in front of Carl's kitchen window. I opened Chopra's book and started reading about "Stage Five," the stage in which we supposedly become co-creators of our lives by following our own inner inspiration.

While mulling this idea over, I looked out the window at the office building across the street. It was a pretty narrow street, so I could easily see the people sitting in their offices, typing away under fluorescent lights and pausing every so often to answer the phone or talk to a coworker who appeared at their office door. The professional atmosphere reminded me of the interview process I was going to have to go through in applying for the job at JMU. I was going to have to put on the suit and heels I'd bought for my first interviews three years ago and parade around imitating someone who wanted to win the admiration of the professional philosophy community. The thought of it made me sick to my stomach.

That's the moment in which I finally realized that this "dream job" was not a dream job at all. Not for me. It was a job very much like the one I'd had for two years at Brandeis—a job that, while excellent by the standards of academia, by the end had me falling over myself to get out of it. Driving out of Massachusetts in that U-Haul had been one of the most liberating days of my life. Did I really want to put myself in another situation where my most frequent dream was one of escape?

Coincidences, I decided then and there, were not always signposts. Sometimes they were *tests*.

Not long after this, I came across a passage in one of Julia Cameron's books where she mentions this other, contrasting function of synchronicities. But that day in New York, I didn't need Cameron's guidance. I felt the truth in my gut. For two days in New York, I'd been avoiding Washington Square because I knew that, if I entered the neighborhood of NYU, I'd feel obligated to turn in my application. A deep part of me—a part of me that often directed my actions below the level of conscious awareness—would simply not allow it. This job advertisement, I concluded, was nothing more than a way for my unconscious to reassure my rational, logically minded self that I had no reason to regret leaving philosophy.

On my last full day in the city, I decided I wanted to enter my old neighborhood in safety. So I took the manila envelope of application materials out of my backpack. When I went out for the day, I left it lying on the floor of Carl's apartment.

From the Financial District, I walked up Broadway all the way to NYU, where I went into my favorite coffee shop from my grad school days and ordered an Americano and an oatmeal raisin cookie. I pulled a stool up to one of the bar tables near the front window, and I spent three luxurious hours writing, and giving not a single thought to philosophy. Instead, I wrote about homeschooling. About what it had felt like in ninth grade to finally have control over my own schedule and to have the freedom to pursue my own interests exactly as I saw fit. In my first semester at home, I'd written a novel, learned to program in C++, and compiled a dictionary for American Sign Language in which you could look up signs by their hand shape. As I was writing about that feeling of boundless creative energy—very similar to what I was experiencing in the present moment—a fire truck pulled up outside the coffee shop, strobe lights whirling. I wasn't worried, as there were always false alarms in the NYU buildings. What caught my attention was the identifying number painted on the side of the truck: 33. I smiled and nodded. *Of course.*

That night, Carl and I went out for pizza downtown. As soon as we were shown to our table, I noticed that there was a basketball game on TV, and that one of the teams had 33 points. I squinted to see who it was: the Boston Celtics.

"I know you're going to think I'm crazy," I told Carl, "but I have to tell you this thing that's been going on with the number 33." I recited everything for him, from the 33s on the tarmac in Washington to the 33 on the fire truck that afternoon. I also told him about a random 33 Samuel and I had found stenciled on the asphalt in the parking lot outside Samuel's beach house, right next to the spot where we habitually parked during our last month together.

Carl listened well, though I could sense in him the same skepticism I'd had when Samuel first started pointing out 33s to me. "You don't have to believe they're significant," I said. "I just wanted to tell you, so you would know why I laugh every time I see another one." I told Carl, too, about my decision not to submit my application to JMU, prompted by the office building outside his window.

After dinner, we walked back to his apartment. He was an architecture journalist, and I had a casual interest in architecture, so he told me about some of the noteworthy buildings we passed along the way. "This one's Philip Johnson," he said. "1984. He originally designed it for the Federal Reserve, but now it's just random offices."

"Hey," I said, noticing the windows in the upper stories, "that's the one you can see from your apartment, isn't it? That's the one I was looking at this morning."

"You're right," he said.

"And is that the address?" I asked, pointing at the bronze plaque beside the entrance.

"Yep," he said. "33 Maiden Lane."

EPILOGUE

Nine years have now passed since the events of the last chapter. Sometimes that feels like a long time. Other times it feels very short. What is fascinating is how much my life has changed. And yet how the core of it has stayed the same.

A month after the Maiden Lane episode, I went back to France to spend another month with Samuel. We both knew, going in, that this time was the real farewell. I had come to terms with that. Accepted it. But both of us wanted a little more time with one another. And I'm so glad we allowed ourselves to have it, because that last month together turned out to be the most meaningful and intimate period of our entire relationship. I learned so many things about Samuel I had never known. I came closer to understanding what was drawing him into another life apart from me, and when he cried as he told me his stories, I was able to hold him close and offer him some small measure of comfort.

I was also able to share with him my joy and fascination at all the things I was now learning about myself and the world. It was a month full of synchronicities. Of the right books appearing in front of our faces at just the right time. Literally. Once I was in the bookstore, flipping through a book that I was trying to decide whether to buy, when one particular passage of the book jumped out at me, about the research of a certain psychiatrist. I turned back a page to start the section from the beginning and immediately discovered that the psychiatrist was from the University of Virginia. And then the first footnote in that section was footnote 33. It referenced a French translation of this psychiatrist's most important book. I thought to myself, *Maybe they have that book in this store.* I lifted my head, and as soon as my eyes focused on the shelf in front of me, I realized that I was looking *at that very book*. Of course I bought them both.

The whole month was like that. Samuel and I danced, cried, and had some amazing laughs. Most of all, we shared our deep admiration for each other and for the great, mysterious One behind it all.

On the day before I left, Samuel told me the name of the woman that he believed he was now meant to be with. He didn't want to tell me at first. But I told him it would help me. I had told him one day at the beginning of my visit that I wanted to be a part of his story with her, that I wanted to share the meaning that it gave to our separation. If I had to go through this pain, I also wanted to share in their happiness. When I told him that, he cried. Hard. I understood it as being from relief, because I was letting him know that it was really okay for him to go. That he wasn't betraying me. That I really was wishing him the very best for his life. Now, just before flying home, I told him I wanted to know her name so that I could bless her by name—bless them both—in my prayers. And so he told me what it was. And I sent her joy.

Back in the States, I sent Samuel an email that I said he could forward to her if he wanted. In it, I thanked her for being something to Samuel that I was incapable of being, for sharing with him things I was unable to share, for reasons that in the end I could only glimpse and guess at. I don't know if he ever sent it to her, but it is still an accurate reflection of my feelings. That's not to say that I didn't have recurring moments of anger. I'm human, after all. But the great majority of the time, I wish her—and I wish them both together—all the happiness in the world.

The thing is, love does turn out to be enough. It's not enough, maybe, to give us exactly the life we desire. It doesn't follow predictable, easily discernible patterns. But it does have this one predictable aspect: it will always take us somewhere good, even if that place is on the other side of tremendous pain.

I have never once regretted my relationship with Samuel. I have never regretted giving him so much of my heart. He was faithful to what I gave him, to the very best of his abilities, and what we shared was worth immeasurably more than all the hurt we endured.

I sometimes wonder if I knew this was the way things would work out. I remember in the first few days we were together as a couple, when I didn't yet know the seriousness of Samuel's intentions, thinking that, even if this love affair were only a few months long, it would be worth it. I jumped in with both feet and my whole heart, and the result was far more than I ever dreamed of. In a way, I suppose, I lived a bit of my favorite tragic love story, *Out of Africa*. Like Karen Blixen, I lost the man I loved, and the farm in a foreign land where I'd found my independence, but I gained an amazing reservoir of memories. And I learned, most of all, just how much love I'm capable of. Of receiving, yes, but most astounding of all, of giving.

I think some people worried about my ability to move on from my relationship with Samuel. Myself included. Especially since our love was still so strong, and since he continued to say that he hoped we would be together again one day. It sounds like a recipe for agony, for wasting away one's life in waiting. And there certainly were some moments of agony, but I was also given a great gift. One year to the day after the last time I spoke to Samuel, I locked eyes with the man who is now my husband.

Every love story is different. Every relationship causes you to bloom in different ways, to see yourself in a new light and develop your capacity for love in new directions. But I am dazzled to have discovered that it is indeed possible to love two people truly and thoroughly in the same lifetime. My journey with my husband has not been without its bumps—many of them caused by echoes from my past with Samuel. Thankfully, we have also had the benefit of not a few miraculous "coincidences" to help us on our way. But those are a story for another time.

The essential thing is that the unconditional love I felt that one night as I was getting ready for bed is now wonderfully familiar to me. I am constantly learning. Constantly healing. And my heart is wide open, welcoming whatever is coming next.

Acknowledgments

I first began writing this book in 2007, and it's gone through many iterations over the years, including a sprawling five hundred-page version that my friends and fellow writers Debbie, Carl, and Alicia were kind enough to actually *read*. Thank you, guys, for bearing with my early meanderings and trusting that there was a jewel in there somewhere!

In 2011, my memoir writing got a huge boost from Sarah Hepola at Salon.com, when she decided to publish my essay "When my fiancé told me about the other woman." I discovered my audience through that piece. And my voice. Thank you, Sarah, for giving me that chance.

Five years later, in 2016, the manuscript was finally closing in on its current form, and I am thankful for those who read that (blessedly much shorter) version and whose enthusiasm gave me so much pleasure. Thank you to Micaela, Bill, Kathryn, and particularly to my courageous mother. Mom, your encouragement was one of the greatest lifts I got in the whole process of writing this book.

Thank you, too, to those who read the final draft of the manuscript in late 2019: Charlyne, Joyce, and Kellie. Your reactions reassured me that this book was, indeed, ready to go out into the world.

Of course, these acknowledgments wouldn't be complete without an expression of my appreciation for all the people who were a part, not just of the writing of this story, but of the living of it. My journey has been immensely helped by my family—Mom, Dad, Sarah,

Rebecca, Ryan—and by the friends who were listening ears throughout, particularly Alicia, Debbie, and Carl. Thank you, too, to Samuel's father and sister. You will always have a special place in my heart.

To "Samuel": I hope you will be pleased by the way I've told our story. I believe our lives are living proof that there was a higher purpose behind it all, a purpose we are still discovering day by day.

And, finally, to my dear husband: I have never felt more secure than when I am in your arms. Thank you for your extraordinary love and support.

Also by
Sharon Hewitt Rawlette

The Source and Significance of Coincidences:
A Hard Look at the Astonishing Evidence

"A marvelous–and awesome–contribution."
— Larry Dossey, MD, *New York Times* best-selling author of
Healing Words and *One Mind: How Our Individual Mind
Is Part of a Greater Consciousness and Why It Matters*

"A 'must-read'."
— Sophy Burnham, *New York Times* best-selling author of
A Book of Angels and *The Art of Intuition*

"Ground-breaking and one of a kind."
— Dr. Mary Helen Hensley, best-selling author of *Understanding Is the New Healing*, *Promised by Heaven*, and co-author of *Bringing Death to Life*

"Elegantly written, thorough, sophisticated, and nuanced."
— Stephen E. Braude, PhD, author of *Crimes of Reason* and *The Gold Leaf Lady*, editor-in-chief of the *Journal of Scientific Exploration*

www.ingramcontent.com/pod-product-compliance
Lightning Source LLC
Chambersburg PA
CBHW031104080526
44587CB00011B/824